Family Story

by Philip F. McNairy

Greenwich · Connecticut · 1960

GRATEFUL ACKNOWLEDGMENT is made: to the Rev. Frederick W. Kates for permission to quote the prayer by Bishop Brent, p. 2; to Everett Smith for his poem, p. 14; to Dr. Harry Emerson Fosdick for the quotation, p. 20; to Frances Greenleaf Jensen for her poem, p. 39; to Viking Press for the copyrighted quotation, pp. 51-52, from James Weldon Johnson's *God's Trombones;* to Alfred Knopf, Inc., for the copyrighted quotation, p. 67, from Kahlil Gibran's *The Prophet;* to Hodder and Stoughton for the copyrighted poem, p. 107, from G. A. Studdert Kennedy's *The Unutterable Beauty;* to the American Tract Society for the copyrighted hymn, pp. 128-29, by John Oxenham. We have been unable to locate the author or source of *The Victor,* pp. 98-100; if brought to our attention, we shall be happy to make acknowledgment in subsequent editions.

TO CARY, PHIL, JUDY, AND PAT,
WHO HAVE WRITTEN,
IN LETTERS OF LOVE AND JOY,
OUR FAMILY STORY

To the Reader:

Words may open doors of understanding. They may also close minds that are not equipped to wrest meaning from them. Especially is this apt to be true in the Christian Religion.

Many people have been repelled by such seemingly technical terms as Atonement, Redemption, Salvation, Incarnation, the Trinity. Still others have been confused by partial or limited explanations of: faith, sin, suffering, death, love, etc.

To assist us in such difficulties we look for parallel situations in everyday experience which give us clues to understanding. These so-called "analogies" never fully describe the truth we are seeking. They do in part at least illustrate the truth and often provoke our curiosity to search more profoundly the area of thought on which they shed some small glimmer of light.

This book was written for those who stand somewhere between curiosity and agnosticism—not sure what they should believe, nor certain they can believe, yet wishing for Christian beliefs upon which they may establish a living faith. "The Family Story" was in part a series of radio addresses given in Buffalo, New York while the writer was Dean of St. Paul's Cathedral in that city. It draws its analogies from family life. With what amazing frequency we encounter, in home and family, situations that parallel the Divine-Human Relationship, we shall attempt to illustrate in the pages that follow.

This volume is not for the clergy, nor yet for well-informed churchmen. It is for those who are humble enough and eager enough to pray, "Help Thou my unbelief."

PHILIP F. McNAIRY

Table of Contents

PART I

The Family and Religious Truth

*

Shed the bright rays of thy light, O Father, upon this family and household, that every member of the same, made confident by thy guidance, may fulfill his daily duty with pure motives and a gallant heart. Be close to us in times of stress and strain, that our courage and our hope may never fail. Let thy sheltering arm protect us, that we may be valiant in all peril. Turn for us sorrow into joy, darkness into sunshine, death into life; so that when the evening comes and our work on earth is done, we may pass triumphantly into the uplands of fellowship in thy family above; through Jesus Christ our Lord.

—*Charles Henry Brent*

No Place Like Home

WHEN FIRST I saw her she was intensely absorbed in the act of boarding the Hartford-bound train. She hurried along the platform, looking neither right nor left, although occasionally glancing downward. The latter she did with good reason, for her hands clasped, not the usual traveller's luggage, but instead, two smaller hands. At her right marching doubletime beside the woman was a lusty five-year-old boy. On her left, straining to keep the pace, trotted a little girl of three. Here was a traveller with an all-consuming responsibility which she seemed eminently prepared to assume. Her gray slacks would withstand the sticky grasp of an eager child far better than the bright linen dress she might have chosen. Her sling purse dangled safely from a sweatered shoulder, leaving her physically free to concentrate on "Operation Hartford."

On boarding the train she wisely preempted the double seat at the front of the coach, since it offered the most strategic play space in the car for her two charges. Who was she? governess? baby sitter? The events of the next hour were to answer this inquiry eloquently and unmistakably.

Within a few minutes the male member of the trio began exploring his new environment. His search was rewarded. It was not long before he became absorbed in a petite "attraction" on the seat behind him. For a brief interval he was captivated by the flashing eyes and coquettish glances of his new-found charmer. Then suddenly the little stranger changed her tactics. The lips that had smiled a moment ago suddenly, and without provocation, pouted an uncomplimentary remark. Just as suddenly the would-be young Don Juan was transformed into a wounded gladiator. With clenched fist he leaned far over the back of his seat. Before he could strike the intended blow, a soft remark from his "travel-guide" neutralized his anger.

"Sticks and stones . . ." The lad finished the quotation: ". . . will break my bones; but words will never hurt me." Under the therapy of the "soft answer" his fist unclenched. He retired with great dignity to face the reassuring smile of the woman beside his sister in the opposite seat. In a flash I knew for certain what I had previously merely surmised. These two were mother and son—and a wise and dedicated mother she was, at that. How simple it would have been to say to the belligerent boy, "Jim, no, no." But instead of a response to a proverbial parental command, I had witnessed a child's decision. At some earlier time, no doubt, this youngster had seen his mother similarly react to a provocative situation—with head instead of impulse. Vision for his decision had come to him because his parent did more than *point* the way—she was way, truth, and life. A divine principle had taken flesh. How simple, yet how wise is the plan of God that entrusts life in its helpless infancy to human stewards for growth and development. Where is there a better opportunity to fashion a mature adult than in the bosom of a family that accepts as a privilege the divine investment of childhood?

But I was to learn more from these three. When presently a sandwich vender entered the car, crying his wares, the mother bought three with cheese centers. Quite naturally, one would assume—three appetites, three sandwiches. The process of distribution was obviously very simple. But once again this wise young woman took advantage of a situation to drive home in unforgettable fashion an important truth. She raised one sandwich. Immediately from opposite sides of her two expectant hands were extended. With a decisive motion she broke the sandwich into two parts, handing one portion to each child. As she did so, she said emphatically, "We share; we share." Once again this family was living and illustrating an Eternal truth. A battle for possession was turned into a love feast by the love of the giver for each of her offspring. Indeed, it was a kindred love that poured out that day on a Palestinian hillside, when a multitude were "fed" by the Loving One who "took the seven loaves and gave thanks, and brake, and gave to his disciples to set before" (the multitude). Here, in a railroad coach, a family were investigating together the foundation stones for human peace and brotherhood. When the material things of life are accepted by their recipients not as possessions, but as gifts of love from the Giver of "every good and perfect gift" to which all are entitled, there will be no more wars. Theft and robbery will cease. Exploitation will vanish. Discrimination will be outmoded. At the heart of brotherhood is the acknowledgment of Fatherhood. Once again, this is a family discovery. The home is the proving ground for the missiles of Spiritual Power. Every hour of every day in a Christian home the members of it have opportunity to illustrate again and again the way of God with a man—indeed, with all mankind.

Little boys, after eating, must satisfy other needs. Our young traveller was no exception. Having located the proper room, his mother granted him permission to "go" with this admonition: "Come right back and don't touch anything." After an interval far longer than ordinarily necessary, the boy returned, obviously the victim of his own disobedience. Noisily expressing his discomfort, he was attempting to rub liquid soap from his face and eyes. The mother, with sternness observed, "This is what happens when you don't obey the rules." Then resolutely she marched him into the same "room" and removed the smarting fluid with fresh water. For the next twenty miles, our juvenile explorer sat gladly within the sheltering, forgiving arm of the one who had "ordered, permitted, suffered with, and saved" her beloved offspring. Who, watching this drama, could not see in it a pinpoint application of the Divine Law: "Choice has its consequence"? Judgment, human or divine, would indeed be tragic except for the fact that Love is on the throne, and Forgiveness is at the bench. The wrath of the mother at the child's disobedience was the righteous indignation of love. So the Loving Creator has decreed, given freedom, permits consequence (rather than remove the privilege of choice). Similarly, out of Love, God is wrathful, suffers for us and with us, redeems and restores us to oneness with Himself, when, in the adult version of the penitent boy, we want and seek that At-one-ment.

I left the train, realizing more fully than ever before that there is no place in the world so well equipped as the home to teach, illustrate, and live, in simple everyday experience, the truths of the God-to-man relationship. So often they are obscured for the average person by wordy definition and technical terminology. Here in the home is a language of action perfected from the letters of life that surmounts such barriers. The loving outreach of a mother's arms can become for the beloved the outward and visible sign of the Everlasting Arms. How great the privilege! How great the responsibility!

There's no place like home to learn about Love, Freedom, Faith, Sin and Forgiveness, Grace, the Cross, Life, Death, Judgment and Redemption. "There's no place like home."

In the following chapters we shall attempt to point out some of the great Christian concepts as they appear, or are implied, in the everyday experiences of the family. It is my hope that as you read further, the simple analogies to Christian thought which we have attempted to present, will enable you to write your own family story with greater insight and with a deeper sense of the spiritual implications of everyday experiences.

Birth

THE INCARNATION

"IT'S A BOY!" There is much excitement tonight in a house on our street. Father telephoned the good news this afternoon. Now even the youngest members of the family know about it. Little Susie is all atremble. She has been telling neighbors—playmates—the postman—the paper boy. And why not? The birth of a baby is an event to bring happiness and human interest to any family. Susie had been observing with wonder the freshly papered room at the end of the hall. Just yesterday she had peeked at the new crib. How could a baby sleep in that tiny thing? The baby bath was another mystery. She carefully noted tiny blankets folded on the bed. She had even wanted to borrow them for her doll. Now all these curiosities were suddenly taking on new meaning. The baby would be home on Christmas night.

The birth of a child has a significantly transforming effect on any home so blessed. Suddenly there is a new purpose for the parents, a new and unifying center of attention for the entire family. Children who were rivals for toys and privileges are transformed for a time by the new *Someone*. Mother and father see with fresh understanding the nature of their love for each other, of which this little creature is the outward and visible sign. Lives that have been geared to pay check and possessions discover a higher value in this helpless and economically worthless infant whom they have had some part in creating.

Now if ever, the Purpose of God becomes clearer. Divine Love has become intermingled with human love. As a result, man and wife are the recipients of a priceless gift. What a wonderful compliment to these two ordinary humans— that God should entrust to them so tremendous an assignment! The responsibility is staggering. What foundation for character this child shall have, they must give. Whether this tiny babe shall grow to be a self-centered, heartless, craven, or a noble man of principle and faith, capable of love, and worthy to be a citizen and a man depends upon the care and training he shall have through his childhood years in this very house. With the awareness of their great privilege, there is reborn a deepening sense of responsibility. They look backward as well as forward. What about Susie and Dick? Have *they* had the kind of beginning which will bring them to healthy and effective maturity? Perhaps mother and dad can make a better start with this new little one. And it isn't too late to make a few constructive changes in their treatment of the other two. Just ahead of them are the dreams, the hopes, that these children will bring honor to the family, perhaps help to build a better world than the one several generations of adults have come so close to wrecking. Just now mother is absorbed in the new miracle she holds so tenderly. If the thoughts of her heart could be transposed into words, she might say with Elizabeth, who beheld another even more singularly blessed:

My soul doth magnify the Lord, and my spirit hath
   rejoiced in God my Saviour.
For He hath regarded the lowliness of His hand-
   maiden.

It is the birth of that baby, the Holy Child, which casts its healing spell upon the believing families of the earth. Centuries pass, yet the story of the Babe of Bethlehem never grows old. One cannot help but feel that even in those lands shut in by the iron curtain the Spirit of *Babouska,* the little gift-bearer, will lighten the heavy hearts of the oppressed. Who knows? Perhaps even the men of the Kremlin recall that Babe who brought life and the power of peace to those who received Him.

Thank God there are many lands still, where men are free to warm their hearts at the shrine from which so much of their culture has sprung. In Mexico the festivities begin early. The Birth of the Christ Child is brought anew in song and story. Those strangely decorated pottery vessels called *piñata* will be hung in the doorways, awaiting the blows of children—until one more vigorous than the others will send it crashing to the floor, spilling its contents of fruits, candies, and gifts in all directions. What a scramble to recover them! How delighted shall the children be!

Or, think of the children in Holland, merrily circling the youngest child as they bid St. Nicholas welcome in their song.

Then again it may be Syria where windows are ablaze with pinpoints of light—Christmas candles to light the Christ Child's way. How many curious customs and legends have grown around the greatest event in history. Think of the Swedish children feeding the birds, sharing their joy with the lesser creatures of God. Remember Jule-Nisse, the dwarf of Denmark who cares for the children, bringing them gifts. How many an author has borrowed from his story the *Krist-Kind* legend of Germany: The little stranger who walks the lonely streets looking for someone to give him shelter and food. Then, finding kindness and the will to share, he suddenly becomes the Prince of princes before them. As the spectators look in awe and wonder, the angelic chorus hails the Infant Christ.

How many a child has been rocked to sleep while a mother's lullaby echoed the refrain of a Christmas carol.

Perhaps in your own living room on Christmas Eve an evergreen tree is suitably covered with shimmering ornaments. It recalls the legend of the forest that bloomed at Christmastime. Here again is the love of infancy and new life, reflected in these green symbols of nature, while the land carries its winter burden of snow and dormant life. Here is the expectant hope that God, in His love, will transform our winters of land and of heart into the spring of new life and joy. What shall we say of these legends? Is the whole story of the birth of Christ a fantasy or a symbol? Some would regard it so. But in everyday experience it is fact that begets fancy. Greatness produces folklore. Great events accumulate legends about them which neither prove nor disprove the event, but illustrate the truth. So the Birth of Christ is the great event that has produced, in retrospect, the lore of shepherds and wise men, as well as many others not included in the gospels. They neither prove nor disprove, but illustrate the fact that "God was in Christ reconciling (winning) the world unto Himself."

And outlasting all these Christmas customs there is the creche with the little figures representing Mary, Joseph, the shepherds, the Magi, and the infant Jesus, instituted, we are told, by St. Francis that humankind might never forget the simple and the humble means God chose to bring into our world the Gift of Himself.

The more we observe the timelessness and the scope of this great heritage of ours, the more it becomes evident that only Divine Wisdom could have fashioned so effective an instrument for His visit to earth. There may be those who still ask why infancy should have been the means of God's

Revelation. Little man with his little mind shall never know all of the whys of God, except they be made known to him by the Heavenly Father Himself. Yet even we, who have the great record of those who "saw and believed," may find the answers to a great many of our questions by means of knowledge and reason.

1. Why should the great Creator of the World bother with us at all? The fact remains that He does—He replenishes life, provides us with food and shelter, heals our sickness, mends our broken hearts. Even the most primitive people have sensed a God of Power. The Hebrew people grew to know a God of Purpose and of Goodness. Still it remained for God alone to make Himself known to us as a God of Perfect Love. But how could man know this for sure? How can we know anything except we have the capacity to understand by experience? We *do* understand the love that draws a man to a woman, which culminates in marriage. We *do* understand the love that has some small part in the birth of a child. Since it is His Love which we need to experience, what better way could God have chosen than to come to us on the level of our ability to comprehend? In the "Birth and Life of Christ" William Temple said, "We have God in terms of men." God has come down to our level of experience.

Perhaps, sir, you have satisfied your urge to be a locomotive engineer by buying Junior, aged six, a model train for Christmas. When the newness wears off *your* hobby, you may give it to the boy for his amusement. "Here son, is a train. You run it." See how bewildered the little fellow is. He knows nothing about assembling track, about transformers, about electrical connections. Given this toy under these conditions, he will soon destroy it or turn away from it to something he understands. If you are wise, you will get down on the floor where he is. You will guide his hands and his mind in the first assembly of this little instrument. You will show him how to connect the wires to the track. A new interest may at that moment be born of understanding. Soon your son will be running his own train. The words "train," "transformer," "switch" have taken visible meaning.

This is the method God has chosen to teach us what it really means to be a man. We speak of the great act in which He did that as The Incarnation. Instead of hovering over the mountaintops and frightening us with thunder and storm into fearful obedience or rebellion, He has come down to us in such a manner that we CAN understand. "And the Word was made flesh and dwelt among us and we beheld . . ." Christ said to men such as you and me, "I am the Way—follow thou me," and they followed Him, until the day they were ready to accept personal responsibility for life as God intended it. Do you recall the conclusion of one of the disciples who had thus been trained? He declared, "God so loved the world that He gave His only begotten Son, that whosoever believeth in Him should not perish, but have everlasting life."

2. God chose birth as His means of entering our experience for still another reason. Like the birth of a child, the awareness of God must spring from within us. It may linger in the matrix of our minds for awhile as a tiny feeble thing. It must grow within us until it is ready to burst upon the world in character and life. There is a glow of affection which radiates from Bethlehem and mellows many a hardened person for a few hours a year. Who knows? One day it may start a flame even in the minds of cold war specialists, moving them to seek a real peace. The peace of the world calls for more than sentimentality. Character is a deeper thing than a Christmas dinner or a necktie. Christ the Babe did not alter human life. It is Christ the man who did that. In a short poem Everett Smith has expressed this conviction:

The world can meet at Bethlehem.
Everybody stands hushed before the helpless Christ,
    wrapped in swaddling bands.
It is not hard to spare the gifts that fill a baby's
    hands.

The World can meet at Nazareth.
Everybody turns gladly to a boy Christ, who loves,
    obeys and learns,
Who grows into our neighbor Christ, a working-
    man who earns.

Anyone may meet the Christ in any town he knows.
Christ changes lives and rescues cities where He
    reigns and grows,
But none can keep a living Christ wrapped in swad-
    dling clothes.

We can only guess what became of the shepherds and
wise men who worshipped Christ the Babe. But we don't
have to look far to see the terrific impact upon all life that
was made by the disciples who knew and worshipped Christ
the Saviour of the world. The goal of their lives, the reason
for their efforts, the explanation of their character, the faith
capable of making them martyrs—these are the gifts of
Christ. We today know that to stifle Christian knowledge,
to eliminate God and the worship of Him for only one
generation, is to bring results that are ghastly. Character and
morality shrivel; love dies; peace becomes a myth. Truth
is abandoned; and life loses its value. This can happen here
in America if we let it. If it should, curse not God when it
happens. Curse the day man wrote this epitaph on the tomb-
stone of our civilization:

Here lies the glory of a people whose final mistake was that they took into their own hands the task of fashioning the purpose and the plan of life.

It is the Spirit which annually unites us in a common tradition of carol and story, and growing to maturity in us is needed in our united effort to establish a world of nations with enough goodwill among men to make peace a reality. Don't wait for angels to sing the song of the heavens. It must be sung out in the lives of such as you and me.

Almighty God, who has poured upon us the new light of thine incarnate Word; Grant that the same light enkindled in our hearts may shine forth in our lives; through Jesus Christ our Lord.

War in the Nursery

ORIGINAL SIN

THERE WAS war in the nursery this afternoon. Just as the bridge game was reaching its peak of interest, the quiet of the living room was pierced by a frightening scream. There followed the distressing sound of small children crying at the top of their lungs. Cards flew in all directions. Chairs scraped. Two anxious mothers arose as one and fairly raced to the children's room. What catastrophe could have befallen their beloved offspring? There on the floor, amid a litter of toys, sat two three-year-olds, both clinging tenaciously to the same toy soldier, their strident little voices raised in a fortissimo of weeping protest, each crying, "Mine. Mine." It took but a moment to supply a second toy and to make a truce between the youthful combatants. Then the two relieved mothers recovered their poise and returned to their companions, saying, "It was nothing—nothing at all."

Their estimate of this infantile situation was *partly* correct. It is perhaps normal for two children, aged three, to become rivals for the same toy. They were born into the world completely self-centered individuals, and so they will remain until the experience or love of later years forces them to recognize the claims and rights of others. Unless and until they are able to make provision for these claims, there will be many tears and much unhappiness. The incident described was not important in itself, except as it illustrates to every parent that a vital part of his task must be the guidance of his offspring away from infant tyranny toward consideration for others.

These babies, however, bring to our attention a basic condition of life which continues as part of our adult emotional and mental structure. What we *do* about it determines to a very great degree whether we have peace, happiness and freedom, or whether we continue to create unhappiness for ourselves and others. This condition of life we call self-centeredness. Dr. Richard Preston, in his book *The Substance of Mental Health,* illustrates with a cartoon this immaturity and self-centeredness at *any* age. Centered in, yet completely filling, a circle is the outline of a baby. He sits cross-legged, arms folded, a crown on his head. He is king of his little world. There is no room in that world for anyone or anything else but him.

Now let's look at our playpen warriors as they will appear at the age of fourteen. Jim is a big fellow for his age, boisterous and argumentative. He's quite the leader among the boys, especially those weaker than he. Jim likes to make decisions—wants to be the pitcher or the quarterback. He takes pleasure in razzing the awkward members of the team. When the game goes wrong, it's the fault of the outfield or the line. Jim is quite the clown at social gatherings. He has a way of attracting the girls, and he'll tell you so if you give him the opportunity. The toy soldier is gone, but "operation nursery" continues. Self-centeredness is still the key characteristic in his makeup. Jack, the other warrior of nursery days, has developed a different set of characteristics. Jack is now the silent type, uncomfortable in the presence of strangers. A bit on the timid side, he hesitates to try anything unfamiliar for fear of failure. He worries about his grades and unduly about his appearance. He is afraid people will not like him and sometimes imagines that they don't. Jack is a "gloomy Gus," except when he receives praise and affection from his parents or friends.

These two lads are quite different; yet they remain much like the babes who fought for the toy. Each suffers acutely from self-centeredness, and there's trouble ahead for both of them. Each has retained self as the center of his life, and because he has he reasons this way: What *he* likes is good. Persons he dislikes must be bad. Faults he condemns in others he excuses in himself. Principles of right are valid when they enable him to have his way. He questions their validity if they don't seem to benefit him immediately. The world is a wonderful place as long as all goes well with him. When it doesn't, he sulks, complains, or seeks an escape. He measures worth in terms of success. He can't be bothered with religion—"That's only for the weak" (and *he* is not weak) "and the old" (and *he* is not old) "or for children" (and *he* is no child).

This self-centeredness is by no means restricted to teenagers. As we see today, it ripens into trouble for many adults. Everywhere around us is the lust for power; and when in politics it is carried to extremes, we see it produce the demagogue and the dictator. Study some of the world leaders who are always in the headlines, and see how they crave authority, how they demand progress. If a principle stands in their way, they eliminate it. If people oppose them they liquidate them. If history contradicts their course of action, they repudiate it. If God and the worship of Him seems to threaten what they want to achieve, they deny Him and forbid His teachings among the people.

If nations stand in the way of our plan, ruin them; defame them; but don't declare war on them unless there is an overwhelming chance of our success. *Now* self-centeredness has outstripped the individual. It controls him. It made him a gangster, then a boss, then a dictator, then a world figure, then an earthgod. But this is as far as he can go. One day death by suicide or assassination or execution claims him. Gone is the toy soldier. Yet in the emotional center of this "man who would be king," we discover Operation Nursery, stage III, with the same diagnosis—self-centeredness.

Students of religion frequently use a single-syllable word to describe the condition of the man, boy, or child who is victimized by his love and worship of self. The person who sets himself on the supreme throne is the victim of "sin." Man, without any authority other than himself, is a man who cannot see God in the circle of life. Sin is the condition of "man-without-God." It, too, is Operation Nursery.

In most instances, however, self-centeredness does not reach such gigantic proportions. It usually centers on our individual lives and affects us at the points of stress and uncertainty. We find it difficult to keep our sense of balance when reverses come to us:

For example, let us take the case of the business man who for weeks has been planning a vacation. A quick airplane trip is to provide him a maximum of time in his sports paradise, where his closest friends are to join him. But one by one his friends find the trip impossible and beg out. He begins to lose some of the zest for his plans. Then, at the last moment, when he is prepared to go on alone, his flight is cancelled because of bad weather. Our friend decides that he has had enough; he abandons his much needed vacation. In a bad mood he plunges back into his work. His resistance is low; he contracts a germ, and complications set in. The result, a costly and damaging illness, indirectly due to a self that could not meet disappointment in a mature way.

Or perhaps this man is one who has suffered great financial loss. Overnight his securities vanish—stocks, bank account, summer home, town house. Sitting in his apartment, his heart fills with bitterness. There are jobs available, but "certainly a man in my position could not be expected to take one of them." His need becomes more acute. His friends help him for a time. But as they see him becoming more and more dependent upon them, they realize that they are only pampering his pride, and complicating his situation by helping him to avoid reality. He sinks into the depths of his own misery, letting precious years go by until it is too late to start again.

Then again, there is the person who has been victimized by circumstances. His friends misjudge him. He feels the stigma of scorn. He can't take it. How to escape? Get out of town? Drown his sorrows in drink or dope? Become a recluse? Commit suicide? Or, just sit and brood and worry until health of mind and body are impaired and opportunity for vindication is lost.

Dr. Harry Emerson Fosdick once used a verse about a many-legged worm, which is very much like the plight of the self-centered man or woman in difficulty. It went:

A centipede was happy quite, until a frog in fun,
Said, 'Pray which leg comes after which?'
This raised her mind to such a pitch, she lay distracted in the ditch,
Considering how to run.

This is the self with which we have to deal day by day. To give in to it is to be defeated and to fall victim of self-centeredness. It is the most common and dangerous form of Operation Nursery. It is to fall, we say, into *sin*.

There *is* a way to live with oneself. There *is* a way to find strength of will to take the road back. There is a procedure whereby hope and peace of mind may be ours. Again let us turn to an illustration of Dr. Preston's. This time to one which depicts maturity. Once again he draws a circle which this time represents the world. Beneath it is the figure of a man who, together with others, is lifting it. The first step in overcoming self-centeredness is to get out of the center of the circle and begin to direct one's thought and concern to others.

Fulton Oursler tells the story of a young lady who, in a fever of despair, sought her physician for help. She sobbed out her pitiful story of loneliness. He could see that she had long since ceased to care about her appearance. He said, "I want you to go to the beauty parlor and get the most becoming hairdo the beautician can select. Then, I want you to buy the most becoming dress the saleswoman can find in the store. When you have done this, return to my office." It was a very different looking, but still uncertain person who returned a day later. "Now," said the physician, "I want you to go to the youth group at the church this evening. Look for people who appear to be lonely and unhappy. Devote your evening to making them forget themselves." It was the best advice anyone could have given. Within a matter of weeks this young lady had recovered her assurance and had found friends and admirers. She regained her self-respect. Within a reasonable length of time, she was happily married. What had she done? She had permitted her physician to direct her attention to something bigger than herself. But first, she had had to accept herself and to have faith in her doctor's remedy.

We need to go a step further in our search for maturity. Let me ask you a question. What is the opposite of self? Another. What other person can you find who has the capacity to receive all of your attention, all of your affection and admiration, all of your love, and strengthen you as you give it? Many have found that God is the only adequate answer to this question. "God, unto whom all hearts are open," knows us for what we are. With Him no pretense is possible, no artifice necessary. God, who gave us life, had a long-range plan for the use of these particular gifts and talents which are yours or mine. Are we not missing our real opportunity unless we find out what it is that God intended us to do with them?

How shall we be able to change so completely our direction of life? How can this self-centered, this sinful, creature that I am suddenly become God-centered? Our answer is: "You cannot do it alone, but God can do it. It will take more than time; it will take *you*."

You have to want to be free of the stranglehold of self.

You have to have the need to find something greater than self to claim your interest.

You have to discover that there is never peace or real happiness until you are freed of self. While there are areas of interest such as family, service, hobbies, church, which may afford you opportunity to "lose yourself," what *you* need most of all to understand is that He, who gave you life, health, a mind, a body, a personality, had a nobler motive than His own amusement or ours. He designed us to find happiness through their wider use with and for others.

We need to discover that His purpose truly is our happiness and that His motive is love. Then we shall see that to rebel against Him, to worship self instead of God, is the greatest injustice we can do to our own lives. Our abilities and talents, be they few or many, were not to be buried in the fallow ground of selfish purpose. They belong to all because they belong to Him. Sometime soon, slip into a church in your neighborhood and open the Book of Common Prayer to the 8th Psalm (p. 350). Read it as if you were asking the question, "What is man that thou art mindful of him and the son of man that thou visitest him?" Let the answer be addressed directly to you: "Thou madest him to have dominion over the works of thy hands." Here is a commission to you, not to play god with the gifts He has given you —your life and ability—but to "have dominion," to control, to dedicate, those gifts in the service of your fellowmen and to the glory of the Giver.

The man who makes these discoveries—and *you* can also—releases himself from the prison of his own small purpose and aim and failure. He lives in the larger life beyond the nursery. He has become a partner in a purpose that is greater than he. He will find a fellowship of persons whose resources for living are mature and strong because they are derived from the same Source as that which made the world.

Nursery toys in infant hands will often bring tears. But the tools of God—faith, hope, love—in the hands of men, who recognize the Giver will bring life worth living. *You* can live with yourself, happily, nobly, triumphantly, when you choose God as the Center of your life.

This Is the Life

GRACE

AT THE WINDOW of the orphanage there is standing an unhappy little boy. This is Danny's first day here and he doesn't like it. There are thirty others like himself, most of them older. He watched them playing ball together after school. He sat with some of them at supper—saw them reach across his plate for that last piece of bread he wanted. All day he had been plied with questions. "What's your name, kid? Where'd you come from? What's the matter—no family?" He had not meant to say Yes when they asked him if he were an orphan. But how could he tell them his father and mother did not want him? The housemother had been kind to him —showed him his room and helped him put away his few clothes. Now this is to be his home—this his bed (first one he'd ever had all to himself)—this his locker. There are five other beds, five other lockers, a table and chairs, four gray walls. Well, at least he is warm and clean; and he isn't so hungry anymore. Yet there is a lump in his throat. He misses those two rooms over the grocery store. He misses his family. But they aren't a family anymore. Daddy and Mom used to leave him with Aunt Bess while the other children were at school. All day long he used to look at pictures or play with his toy soldiers, waiting for Mom to come and take him home. Then, one day Jane came for him, and there were tear stains on her face. She told him he would have to stay with Aunt Bess until Mom came back. He was kind of afraid of Mom. She was all right, except when she sat at the table drinking something. Then she was mean, and she didn't speak very clearly.

All that was a week ago. This morning a strange lady had come to see him. She told Danny she was taking him to a new home. She had his clothes put in a paper sack.

Tonight Danny is alone—so alone. Nobody cares. In all of his four-and-a-half years he has never been so unhappy. Slipping quietly into his new bed, he tries to sleep. Danny's pillow is wet when the nurse comes in to turn out the lights.

In the next six weeks Danny learns a great deal and begins to know the chief rule of the home: "Help with the chores or you won't eat." He can reach for bread with the best of them. And Spike teaches him how to hide food in his locker, just in case "you get hungry at night." Nice kid, Spike.

Then one day the Morrows call at the orphanage; and again, the next day. Mr. Morrow asks Danny how he would like to visit them for the weekend. What fun that had been! The Morrows' home was on the edge of town. Behind the big brown house there was a barn with a real live pony in it. Paul Morrow had taken Danny for a ride. The Morrows kept their house nice and clean. There were lots of rooms in it—and a big fireplace and a piano. Paul and Sandy Morrow seemed to like their parents very much. They liked each other, too. On Sunday morning Danny went to church for the first time in his life. The whole family went with him. In the room they called the chapel there was a picture, on the wall, of a man with some children beside him. The lady told Danny what the words beneath it said: "Let the little children come to me." Somehow that man made him think a little of Mr. Morrow. They both looked sort of kind.

Six happy months later Danny has a new name—Danny Morrow. He has been "adopted." He calls Mr. Morrow "Pop." There is a song in this little boy's heart these days. How wonderful it is to be wanted! People believe in Danny Morrow because they believe in his Dad. They say that he has "a lot to live up to." Danny doesn't quite know what they mean. But if they want him to be the kind of boy who will make his new dad and mother proud of him, he certainly wants to do that. The little thin cheeks have grown chubby. The look of fear is gone from his eyes. He scarcely remembers the old life over the grocery store or at the orphanage. He is a new boy, with a new purpose for living. Think of all that has been done for him! Since he learned to say his prayers, he says "thank you" to God every day for making him so happy. Danny the orphan has become Danny Morrow in fact. The wonder of it all is this: He didn't earn the new place. It wasn't because he was good. He is here because the Morrows love him; because they know how much he needs a home and family.

The changes which took place in the life of Danny Morrow have been occurring on another level of experience in the lives of many people for nearly two thousand years. The story of the Christian life runs parallel to our family story. The person who has become a Christian has become a member of a great new family by adoption, bound together by ties of love for the heavenly Father and united in brotherhood with all others who call Him Lord. The Christian can leave loneliness behind. He has a new identification and a new value among men of similar belief. He has found a new and deeper happiness. He has found a new way of living and a new reason for it.

Once there lived a spiritual orphan named Saul. This victim of a heartless system of rules and laws found, to his amazement that he was drawn by an irresistible Love into the family of Christ, which once he thought he hated. He became a completely different person. He was given a new name, "Paul." He described in one sentence the change that took place in his life: "If any man be in Christ he is a new creature." His own life is the proof of his statement. Instead of living to persecute, he began to live for the purpose of bringing to others the real meaning of life. Instead of being a lonely and hated man, he became loved, respected, an inspiration to men. Instead of fear and bitterness, he found joy in his new life and work. He himself was that "new creature."

How often we overlook this description of what it really means to be a Christian. The common consideration of a follower of Christ is in terms of what he does rather than of what he is. He is thought of as one who tries to follow the example of Jesus, who talks about the Golden Rule and the brotherhood of man, or attends church, or reads the Bible. Even more commonly, a person who does much good and helps others is called by some a "Good Christian." Most certainly this is the behavior we would expect of a Christian. But a person need not be a Christian to meet these requirements. A good Jew or a good Mohammedan might do the same, if he lived in a society where these are the accepted standards of good citizenship.

A young mother once said in great earnestness to her pastor, "I am not concerned about whether you teach my child religion. I expect you to help me teach him to be a good citizen." Of course, she was thinking of good citizenship according to the American standard. What she had forgotten was the fact that the American standard, at its best, is less than the Christian standard of behavior. Suppose the American standard should become unpopular. Suppose a new government should close churches, forbid Bibles, abolish the Community Chest, and take away all right of the individual to help his fellowmen. What then would be the standard of a good citizen? Christianity is more than a system of behavior.

It is the reason for and the power behind that behavior. Real
Christianity has survived hundreds of years of deliberate
attempt to blot it out and liquidate its followers. The real
Christianity that has swept the world, and been driven back,
and will sweep it again, is more than behavior. It is life—
a new life. The Christian man has become a new creature.

 1. Christianity begins with a great belief. What brought
Danny into the Morrow family was a matter of belief—their
belief in him, and his trust of them. Without it, there would
have been no adoption. The Christian begins with the great
belief in God's love for him. God has made known His great
Love and confidence in the man through Jesus Christ. The
Christian believes that he can do his best and fulfill his real
purpose in life only as he establishes a constant relationship
with God. For a man, such a relationship, apart from the
family of believers is impossible. Whether he realizes it or
not, God, "who sets the solitary in families," has created us
as social beings. We are incapable of real spiritual development and happiness apart from one another. But it is only
as we become one with the spirit and purpose of God—as
we become "adopted sons" in His great family of believers—
that we become capable of living together successfully.

 2. Real Christianity is a response to the Love of God. It is
not the doing of a series of good deeds and pious acts to win
favor. Danny did not become a member of the Morrow
family because he had earned the privilege. This "grace"
was his because of his need of it, and because of the desire
of his new parents to share their lives with him. A Christian
cannot possibly earn God's favor because of human goodness. The Christian family is not a society of the near-perfect
upon whom God showers compensating favors. It is a company of people who, although they know they do not deserve
it, have been blessed by the Love and *Grace* of God through
Christ. He wants to share His Great Life with them because

they so desperately need it. When the man discovers this great fact that God accepts him despite what he is, he can never do enough to be worthy of so great a favor. But at least he can spend his life trying.

Dr. Theodore Wedel suggests this comparison. Suppose a man quarrels with his wife. In an attempt to re-win her favor, he buys a dozen roses and presents them to her. Without talking it out, without repentance and forgiveness there can be no reconciliation. But suppose the man discovers he is already forgiven. Then, ten dozen roses will never begin to express his joy. Now he buys them, not as a bribe, but as a thank offering. Such is the relationship of the Christian with God. He knows that he cannot bribe God by human good deeds into favoring him. For God has already blessed him with forgiveness and love, with life and the provisions for it, with hope and the reason for it, with a mind and a soul and the power to use them for good. Therefore his worship becomes thanksgiving. The primitive man cowered in fear on his "sacred hill," performing religious acts that were hideous and inhuman, thinking thereby to incur God's favor and forestall his wrath. The Christian is a free man—free of such haunting fears, free of such distorted concepts of God, free to live and love and worship as a child of God "by adoption and grace." He is no longer the doer of pious acts for fear of what will happen if he does not. Personal goodness is the only logical response to God he can make. Worship is the action whereby additional spiritual strength for service comes to him. His good works are the natural extension of the joy that is his, which comes from God's willingness to share the Divine Life with His children.

3. The Christian now has a new responsibility which he personally undertakes—that is, to live worthy of the new name he bears. His wife cannot do this for him. His children cannot do it for him. His money cannot do it for him. His clergyman cannot do it for him. He wants to fulfill that responsibility personally. Unlike our human family, the Christian family is an ever-growing family, seeking to bring others into this loving relationship with Christ its Living Head. What God did for me, He does for all men. Therefore all are precious in His sight. To him for whom Christ died, regardless of his race or national origin or station in life, I have an inescapable obligation. It is my privilege to carry the good news of this relationship to others. I want them to have what I have found. I want them, too, to be more than imitators of the man with a belief. I want that belief to be the everlasting fountain of *their* lives. I want them, too, to learn to express their thanks to God. I want them with glad hearts to say to others, "This is the life, *the Christian life.*"

O Lord, our heavenly Father, Almighty and everlasting God, who has safely brought us to the beginning of this day; Defend us in the same with thy mighty power; and grant that this day we fall into no sin, neither run into any kind of danger; but that all our doings, being ordered by thy governance, may be righteous in thy sight; through Jesus Christ our Lord.

Rush Hour

FAITH

It could happen in any city, any weekday between four and five-thirty in the afternoon. It happens every hour of every day in Minneapolis at the intersection of Hennepin and Lyndale Avenues, commonly known to residents as the "bottleneck." Here traffic from six directions converges on a point of potential impasse, without benefit of traffic lights and seldom with the assistance of traffic policemen. The cautious drivers, with swivel necks, must dodge the ruthless and the daring, while the timid, inching their way into this maelstrom of metal and human urgency, create bumper to bumper chains of irate commuters whose profane horns provide the chorus for solos of screeching tires. From this motorist's nightmare one emerges dripping with perspiration, aware of his ulcers, and frequently with a newly acquired reason for a visit to the collision service department of his garage.

Not infrequently one observes in this mechanized madness the eighth wonder of the world—a pedestrian with fortitude enough to commit his body to the mercy of these "guided missiles" as he seeks to pass from curb to curb.

At this particular moment our eyes are glued to one such courageous soul who descends into the line of fire calmly and cautiously, but with every sinew tense, eyes and ears alert to the danger from every side. She chooses the blanks in each clip of motor projectiles to make her way, lane by lane, across the street. Her progress is impeded and her task complicated somewhat by the fact that she bears a double responsibility. For at her side, scarcely waist high, trudges a child, seemingly unaware of the tension and of the danger surrounding him. He is by contrast relaxed, almost casual—not a worry in the world; for his hand is firmly enclosed by that of his mother, whom he trusts implicitly.

Here is a childhood version of an Act of Faith. We notice certain aspects of it which we would do well to remember. First, *faith is not blind trust.* Quite to the contrary! Several years of day by day experience have prepared this child for this rush-hour episode. He has been fed by his mother, clothed, carried, scrubbed, and combed by her. He has known her loving hand and voice as he went to sleep and upon awakening. He has learned she can be firm and corrective as well as gentle and permissive. Above all, he has found her utterly reliable. She has been his comfort in the storm, his source of warmth in cold, his eyes and ears in every situation. It is not by chance or sudden impulse that he is moved to face traffic danger without fear. His diminutive capacity to reason already tells him he is safe, for his mother is at his side. His faith is not blind trust. It is a step into the unknown on the basis of the known. It is built upon facts, the chief of which being that he knows his mother loves him, wishes, above all, his happiness and well-being. Second, *faith is an act of the will.* It is not inertia. It is decision. It is action that results from beliefs. This child would have refused to cross the thoroughfare by himself; or should he have attempted it, he might have been crushed after the first step. Because of his belief in his mother, because he knows her so intimately to be trustworthy and dependable, because he believes in her love of him, he places himself, in

complete obedience and by an act of his will, in her care.
Third, *faith is the surest way to inner peace.* How unlike
the drivers of the automobiles this little child is. They must
rely entirely upon their own skill and judgment. They must
take a chance upon the dependability, indeed the sobriety of
the drivers of the other cars. The child in rush hour traffic
is a single point of calm at the center of the storm. In far
greater danger than the auto-borne, this child's mind has
found a security (limited as we know it to be) to sustain him
inwardly in this hour—his mother.

Translate this child's experience to life in general. Faith
is our greatest bastion against the hazards and the wear and
tear of life. Yet, like the youngster's faith, it must be forged
in similar fashion if it is to serve a man in the "rush hour of
life."

FAITH IS NEVER BLIND

Faith is never blind, or else it is foolishness and not
faith. Young lovers will face the unknown future together
with amazing confidence—with far more of it, in fact, than
we think warranted by their youth and inexperience. They
take the step together into tomorrow not despite what they
don't know, but because of what they *do* know of each other.
An employer may decide to engage an inexperienced graduate. Is he taking a great risk in "playing a hunch"? Not in
his estimation. First, he has made a thorough investigation
of the novice: training, grades, character, interview, aptitude
tests, physical, mental and emotional examinations. Then
comes his act of trust. He will face the unknown on the basis
of the known. When one is bidden to "have faith in God,"
blind trust is never implied. The Christian means by this
statement, not a commitment in blind ignorance to any kind
of a god. He means the confident dedication of body, soul,
and mind to the God made known to us in Jesus Christ—

for this life and the life to come. God, whom twenty centuries of men and women by the millions have trusted, worshipped, and given their lives to serve, is no untried flash in the pan. He is more than a "something there." He is no "last resort" or "rabbit's foot" or "wishful thought." He is no genii who appears in emergency's hour. They who have put their trust in Him have come to know Him through the day by day experiences of life—in the calms as well as the storms. They have come to know Him through the Holy Bible, through other lives spent in companionship with Him. They have seen His work and felt His presence in all the seasons of life—at birth, in growth, in recovered health, in death. Parents have watched his "greater miracle" of "turning milk into muscle." They have felt His compassion in the recovery of a sick child. They have faced the "rush hours" of life—sickness, joy, success, failure, love, sorrow—fortified by Strength not of their own creation. They have seen death, not as a blind alley, but as a horizon. Because they are confident of His love, they understand His wrath, even as it is their own love for their children that expresses itself indignantly at juvenile rebellion. They have felt in some small measure the Cross; for they have suffered with and for their own beloved—yea, have been ready to shed their own blood for them. For such as these, Faith is a confident step into the unknown because of the Known. God is known to them to be utterly reliable.

FAITH IS AN ACT OF THE WILL

I recall an occasion of illness that culminated for me in an appendectomy. How can I forget that night of persistent and crippling pain! Toward morning we sent for the diagnostician who promptly sent for the surgeon to whom he regularly referred such cases. I remember their discussion of my case and their rather disconcerting conclusion—"Surgery—the sooner the better!" Under such circumstances the mind races through the facts at hand. Who is this strange man who so nonchalantly makes an appointment to sever my body? He is a well-known surgeon, to be sure. Mayo-trained—brilliant army record—staff member of the leading hospital—Churchman—huge practice. These are reassuring facts. However they are not totally trust-inspiring to one who reluctantly anticipates surgery for the first time. Two other factors weighed heavily in my decision: The physician I knew so well had confidence in this surgeon. As the latter left my bedside, I was struck by his kindly concern for me as a person. *That did it.* Then came the act of the will. "All right doctor, I'll be there. I'm in your hands." Here, at another level of human experience, is faith in action. Like the child in rush-hour traffic, this step into the unknown was made on the basis of the known. It is commitment. It is surrender. It is an act of the will.

How much the more do we need, in the rush hours of life, to come to a first-hand knowledge of, and personal acquaintance with, the Great Physician, "The Lord and Giver of Life." It is a great decision we make with head as well as heart, when in truth we pray, "Into Thy hands I commend my spirit." He whose compassionate Power has given sight to the blind, hearing to the deaf, mobility to the enfeebled, life to the dead—Jesus Christ is our Door from the known to the Unknown—"He that hath seen me hath seen the Father". . . "Into Thy hands . . ." I have thought many times since, if I will entrust my body to a surgeon so little known to me, how much more confidently I ought to trust my life, body and soul, to God whom I have known all my life.

FAITH IS THE WAY TO INNER PEACE

Our greatest insecurities are likely to come from the fact that we feel called upon to pit our capacities single-handedly against the unexplored and the unknown. This type of situation may for a time be a challenge to some—to an explorer, scientist, or new salesman. Yet the salesman reaches the point where he needs and uses the promotional resources and the reputation of the company. The explorer is grateful he can rely on his Geiger counter and for his safety, on the instruments of meteorology; and in the last extreme, he has his compass. The scientist is grateful for the research and experimentation of others. Yet these are temporary resources which in themselves suggest the first intimation of a man's need for strength beyond himself. Suppose a depression erases sales opportunity, or a landslide leaves the explorer wounded and maimed, or surgery discloses a deep-seated incurable ailment in the scientist. But a child at rush hour faces death itself with a calm born of a simple trust that eliminates for him even the consideration of his danger. "Such trust have we through Christ to God-ward . . ."

It is this confident dependence upon God which brings to a man inner peace for the "rush hours" of life. The Christian's primary concern is that he shall be able to face life unafraid and wrest from whatever circumstances it presents the best, instead of the worst. Because he has come to know and love God, and knows he is himself loved, he is delivered from misreading in life's "reverses" a sign of disfavor. He accepts its joys and triumphs, as well as its daily blessings, not as evidence of his own virtue, but of God's gracious goodness. He faces life with the clear knowledge that whatever happens to him, even death itself, God can, will, and does transpose into good, because of His very nature and purpose. Such are the beliefs upon which faith is established. Such are the convictions that for the Christian make possible his commitment. Like a great hand extended to a "child" in rush-hour traffic, he feels the supportive Strength that brings him peace of soul. Faith cries out: "I am persuaded that neither death nor life . . . nor things present nor things to come, nor height nor depth, nor any other creature shall be able to separate us from the love of God which is in Christ Jesus, Our Lord."

O Most loving Father, who willest us to give thanks for all things, to dread nothing but the loss of thee, and to cast all our care on thee, who carest for us; Preserve us from faithless fears and worldly anxieties, and grant that no clouds of this mortal life may hide from us the light of that love which is immortal, and which thou has manifested unto us in thy Son, Jesus Christ our Lord.

Strength Through Suffering

THE OTHER DAY, quite unexpectedly, Bill Strong had been called to the plant office. He was scarcely able to believe the message that was delivered to him. He muttered, "Thanks," and headed for the door and the parking lot. In a matter of minutes he was maneuvering his car through traffic to his destination, the hospital. His wife! "Emergency surgery!" And, "Yes, Mr. Strong, floor three. Ask the nurse." He had arrived there just in time to see a nurse wheeling a litter emerge into the hall. He was reassured at the smile on Mary's face. Her voice was weak, but very certain. "Everything will be all right, Bill. Say a prayer and wait for me. I'll be back soon. Don't worry."

Two hours! They were the longest Bill had ever spent! He scarcely noticed a similar stretcher leave the room across the hall. He had called his rector; then looked at his watch for the n-th time. Now he paced the hall. Then again he was in the empty room. His eyes fell upon a little book, opened casually on the table. He read the familiar words. "The Lord is my shepherd, I shall not want. . . . Yea, though I walk through the valley of the shadow of death, I will fear no evil, for thou art with me . . ." Mary had been reading this. She had said, "Everything will be all right." Bill read on: "Surely goodness and mercy shall follow me all the days of my life." Goodness and mercy.

His reading was interrupted by the reappearance of the nurse. "The surgery has been successful!" With trembling knees he sank into the bedside chair. How fortunate they had been to have this fine hospital and the best surgeon in town. But there was more to it than this. If a man could trust a life so dear to him to a doctor he only knew by reputation, surely the Great Physician, "The Lord and Giver of Life," would know what to do in a case like this. Mary believed it. There was a clipping in her Prayer Book.

"God does not give us strength for worrying; We
    cast our care on Him,
Then snatch it back—as if the hand that formed
    the universe
Could not alone control our little day
So we go stumbling on—and do not see that our
    own clouds of doubt obstruct the light,
And cannot understand why—wearied with the
    burden of our fears
We fail to find the way."
Frances Greenleaf Jensen

All this was three days ago. Tonight Mary had met Bill in the hall. She had had a rough day, but you would never know it to look at her. The nurse had said that she was a wonderful patient. As they turned into the room, the signal light across the hall flashed. As the nurse hurried in, an imperious voice was asserting itself. "Nurse, call my doctor. I can't stand this pain." And then, "What have I done to deserve this?"

Here are two patients with similar ailments; yet one can "take it" and the other cannot. Some people who appear to be strong when health is theirs go to pieces under stress.

The things which once made them self-sufficient are suddenly gone. They are terrified, or depressed and troubled. They try to compensate with demands for their feeling of helplessness. They wish now they knew more about faith and prayer, and about God. "What kind of a God is He? What does He want of me? What have I done?" Perhaps they even see this affliction as a foreshadow of that dread day when mortal life for them will lose all its meaning. So the final fear seizes them and does its best to retard convalescence. Yet across the hall, these words are recited: "I will fear no evil—He restoreth my soul."

Once a man who had endured more than the average of bodily pain sat in his prison cell, writing letters. He wrote with an uncertain scrawl, for the light was going from his eyes. He wrote in haste, not knowing when his executioners might come for him. "Be strong in the Lord and in the power of His might. . . . He said, unto me, 'My grace is sufficient for thee, for my strength is made perfect in weakness.' Most gladly therefore will I glory in my infirmities, that the power of Christ may rest upon me. For when I am weak, then am I strong." Struck down and blinded on the road to Damascus, this man had been deprived in an instant of all his resources. Power, riches, influence, knowledge— none of these could help him. Nor could anything help him until he came face to face with the fact that he *needed* help. Then it was possible for God to reach through the shattered curtain of human pride and heal that life. Paul found *strength* through weakness. This is the hope that God holds out to every sufferer. When a man knows he is weak and admits it to himself, he has taken the first step toward strength. When he is willing to look for help beyond himself, the door to help, both human and Divine, is open. In sickness he may have the strength of clearer vision.

We were speaking about a sick man who cried out in agony, "Why did God do this to me?" His troubled mind seeks an answer. His is one of the common attitudes toward pain. Let us look at some others: There is the dreamer who says, "If I could remake the world, I would eliminate suffering and pain." There is the cynic who snarls his defeat as he cries, "This goes to show you there isn't any real happiness —there isn't any God." Others use illness for self-pity. They enjoy ill health and get their satisfaction out of telling their woes to every listener, urging others to feel sorry for them. Then again there is the man who accepts pain with resignation. A South American Indian tribe reflects the attitudes of several Oriental religions in the saying, "You were born into a world of trouble. Shut your mouth and be quiet and bear it." An early Old Testament idea suggests that pain is punishment for evil. Yet even so primitive a man as Job rebelled against this mistaken notion. It would be difficult to conceive of the good and loving God losing His temper and inflicting pain upon an innocent child. No, there is no enlightenment here. Now, out of our age comes forth the brilliant, but futile and false, idea that suffering and pain do not exist. It reasons thus: "The mind of God can have nothing evil in it. We are part of that mind, therefore suffering and pain are not real." To say that the mind of God is good is correct. *But* to say that there is no suffering is a denial of Christianity. For He who was the best suffered the most, and died in the agony of the Cross—even Christ. To deny this is to deny that "God so loved the world that He gave His only begotten Son for us." So we turn for our answer to Christ, the Way. What did He do about pain? He accepted it. He faced suffering as a fact. Sin and suffering must be met, and a way of life hewn out through them. This is the great fact of the Gospel—that there *is* a Way. The Cross, the worst that man can do, is met by God's triumph in the Resurrection. Suffering is not victory nor is it virtue. Some have thought so, and inflicted it upon themselves and got nowhere. Suffering is *not* the way. But there is a way through suffering to strength.

God does not cause pain. He makes possible its defeat. C. S. Lewis says, "It is men, not God, who have produced racks, whips, prisons, slavery, guns, bombs." Kahlil Gibran says, "Much of your pain is self-chosen. It is the bitter potion by which the physician within you heals your sick self. Therefore trust the physician and drink his remedy in silence and tranquility." Elsewhere this same author says, "Your pain is the breaking of the shell that encloses your understanding; even as the stone of the fruit must break that its heart may stand in the sun, so must you know pain . . ." The strength of Christianity has been in the fact that it leads through suffering to this understanding.

1. Suffering brings to the arrogant man a sense of need. When my life has been stripped of the alleged securities with which I have endowed it—when I discover that all of my little strategies for avoiding disaster are powerless to turn back pain, I look across the hall to that other sufferer, "drinking the bitter potion in silence and tranquility." I ask, "How may I have what she has?"

A visitor in a ward of a London hospital noticed a patient who seemed more calm and peaceful than the others. In talking with the nurse, she discovered that this brave patient was undergoing greater suffering than any man in the ward. The visitor returned to this man's bedside and expressed her admiration for his courage. "It isn't courage," said the sufferer, "it's that"—and he pointed to a little white sign above the head of his bed, which read: "My Grace is sufficient for thee." Here again—"When I am weak, then am I strong." This is the Strength that comes of Faith.

2. The experience of pain can be a great boon to the elimination of needless suffering. It is this which has sent scientists into their laboratories for new types of anesthesia, new surgical techniques. Sickness has given them the strength of compassion. It is because of the agony of mental suffering that physicians have specialized in the study and treatment of the mind and nervous system. It is the understanding born of pain that sends heart ahead of pocketbook as we seek to raise the standard of our mental hospitals above the prison level. It is the agony of those who suffered from the fire, shock, and explosives of war which fills the minds of the compassionate with determination that a better way of settling international differences must be found.

Still there are those today who look at the plight of the people in captive countries and ask, "Why doesn't God stop this needless suffering?" We shall be able to see the problem in its true light if we reduce it to the individual level. Suppose a driver of a car takes a foolish chance on a curve and deliberately crosses to the wrong side of the road. There is a sickening crash, a head-on collision, and five people lie by the roadside, dead or seriously injured. In this instance we would not blame God for this tragedy and ask Him to stop the driving of automobiles. We know the fault lies with man. Our lives, like vines, are interwoven with other lives. Whether they suffer or not depends upon the decisions we make. Whether it involves an automobile or a declaration of war, the fact that there will be innocent suffering is the fault and responsibility of man, not of God. We dare not shift the blame. It is ours. We must face it. But more than this, we must do something about it. This is the supreme confidence God has in us—that we will do something about innocent suffering. Because of the nature of His creatures, endowed with wills capable of deciding for peace, He never loses hope that one day we will reach up and receive His help. He awaits the day when understanding born of our own suffering, and humility born of our own defeats, and determination that springs from our own sense of responsibility, will bring us all to live as children of God.

Thus far we have seen that sickness and suffering are real. They are often man-made. God did not send them to us as implements of His vengeance. They need not prove our undoing. We have noted that the fruit of suffering need not be bitterness, nor resignation, nor defeat. For out of the sickroom have come understanding, compassion, determination, progress and *faith* in God.

An unknown writer observes:

> In pastures green? Not always; Sometimes He who
> Knoweth best, in kindness leadeth me
> In weary ways where shadows be.

If you could know Bill and Mary Strong, you would discover that they have thrust aside the curtain of mystery that seems to enshroud sickness. They did not have to wait until the end of time. They can tell you today how their experience led them to a faith that pays tremendous dividends. Sickness turned their attention to the need of it. They sought help and found it. Today they are different people. They have met the Giver of Life and found Him to be also the Sustainer of Life. Never again will they take God for granted. Never again will they take their fellowmen for granted. They have incurred a debt which they know they can never repay. But they will try. They have endeavored to live in such a way that their home and their lives will reflect the sense of blessing that rests upon them. They will never again fear death. For they came close to it and found it, not an abyss of nothingness, but that the same Lord of Life is there, "keeping watch above His own."

It is perhaps natural that there should mount to the lips of the pain-ridden a question, even as Christ uttered from the Cross, "My God, my God, why hast Thou forsaken me?" It is our human selves crying out for the Divine. It is trust needing to be reassured. Perhaps, one by one, the lights which used to guide us have flickered and seemed to go out. Then look up! There in the twilight you may now see, still shining, the Eternal Light. It is real! It is Power! Through every Cross, God can send a Resurrection. This is the answer which Faith holds out to you and me. We *can* find strength through suffering.

> When through the deep waters I call thee to go,
> The rivers of woe shall not thee over-flow;
> For I will be with thee, thy troubles to bless,
> And sanctify to thee thy deepest distress,
>
> When through fiery trials thy pathway shall lie,
> My grace, all-sufficient, shall be thy supply;
> The flame shall not hurt thee; I only design
> Thy dross to consume, and thy gold to refine.
> —*The Hymnal, 1940* (No. 564)

The Valley of Vision

FAITH IN ETERNAL LIFE

THE FAMILY has spring fever. All morning the roller skates beat their warm-weather tattoo on the sidewalk. There was baseball in the vacant lot. Dad spent two hours, oiling fishing reels and painting tackle, while he should have been cleaning the basement. There was no doubt about it. The usual request would be coming soon. Mother was thankful for her last minute shopping when the word came. It was five-year-old Bobbie, who said it first, "Let's have a picnic."

There were no crowds at the park today. Only the burning crackle of last year's leaves in the fireplace disturbed the silence. An occasional wood sparrow chattered his curiosity at these five pioneers, and snatched a crumb from their evening meal. While the empty basket was being repacked for the journey home, the children scampered over the hills in search of crocus. With their hands full of spring treasures, the children raced back to the table—all but Bobbie. Somewhat anxiously Mother called his name. There was an echo, but no answer. The whole family went into action. Soon the air was so full of the voices of the searchers no one could hear the little cry from the glen below. The smallest child had lost contact with his familiar surroundings. He was alone. Fear shattered his sense of direction. He heard voices, but they seemed to come from everywhere. Choking back the tears, he sat on a fallen log, feeling sorry for himself, wondering what to do. He could not know that friendly fatherly eyes had already discovered the little figure from the ridge above. Soon he was safe in the embrace of his thankful family.

How like a child—to stand helpless before the unknown in this vast, ugly "valley of despair!" How like the adult—to let reason lead him to the view from above! For the man, this valley held no terrors. He knew its small dimensions. He had often marveled at its beauty and peace. For him it was a "valley of vision." Manhood has learned from many an experience that the view from above can turn his valley of despair into a valley of vision. Often when he has stood, baffled before some difficult problem, the experienced view of a fellow workman has given him the insight he needed. All through life we have learned at each new step that the wise apprentice submits his inabilities to the practiced eye of the master craftsman. This the child will one day learn.

But there is a "valley" within which the seasoned adult is as lost as the little child. It happened to our picnic family. It will one day be your experience and mine. For awaiting the returning family was a telegram on the door. It read: "Mother passed away this afternoon. Funeral Tuesday." Suddenly the strong man has become a lost child. No one within his immediate experience has explored the depths of this unknown. Here, all experience, all vision ceases. So at last it is the man's judgment which must be pitted against death, the untried. He wishes it had not happened. He knows of no reason why death should have overtaken his mother. The best in his experience is right here. There is a tinge of resentment in his sorrow. "But she was so good," he says, refusing to note that that very goodness may be what God has claimed for His own. "But I love her," he cries, never considering that God who gave her life loves her more— "with an everlasting love."

What this man needs in his hour of grief, when he is lost in

his valley of despair, is the knowledge that another ha
traveled this way who now stands on the ridge of eternity
Christ sees all of life, not just our little span.

He says to us, "Let not your heart be troubled." "You
believe in God." He bridged the gap between our darknes
and the light beyond. "I go to prepare a place for you . .
that where I am, there ye may be also."

Our difficulty is this: we do not want to face these ques
tions rationally when life is running smoothly. Others may
be stricken around us, but somehow we travel along in an
imagined immunity. Then, one day, it happens. The bottom
drops out of our world. With emotion in the driver's seat,
we try to make up lost time by attempting the impossible.
In the midst of grief, we try to reason out what has happened. Alas, we cannot. Sorrow is the time for faith that rests
on facts, previously assembled.

How many times the clergyman has wanted some opportunity to help his people to build that faith. But their busy
lives—often too busy, they think, to attend to these things—
do not afford the opportunity. Then, after the blow has
struck, he must try to do the impossible. There are insights
available to us now, which, if we make them our own, may
enable us to turn some "valley of despair" into a "valley of
vision."

The dark cloud of sorrow has its silver lining. Sorrow is
the inescapable consequence of love. Mark well how we wish
that grief might be gone forever. The only possible way to
escape it is to shut out from our lives all love and affection
and live in the desert of aloneness. Fortunately, we are not
content to live in solitude. Love, or the capacity to love, is a
part of our very nature. Here is one of the many ways the
loving God has created us in His own image. It is one of the
unchangeable laws of the universe: No sorrow, no love. Many
times during the course of life we apply this principle calmly
to changing circumstances.

Perhaps the happiest years of family life occur when a child has begun to show signs of his eventual development. High school days have come with all of their enthusiasm and adventure. Just ahead is graduation when, likely as not, the child will forsake the home for college or work elsewhere. A parent would not say, "My child was so good, the brightest in his class; why did he have to graduate?" Even though it means separation we want that child to go on from triumph to triumph. We do not want him to stop here.

Life, in a sense, is a series of graduations. We are content only with those we actually know. Yet we trust our loved one to an uncertain man-made future. But God's order is an order of progress. Death is an upward thrust, not a decline—a graduation to a life of greater possibility and effectiveness. Into that future, Christ has advanced, saying, 'I go to prepare a place for you, that where I am ye may be also." Do we not well to trust Him, who has first claim on our lives, with the future of our spiritual existence?

I wonder whether we sometimes misunderstand sorrow and therefore misuse it.

For whom are we sorry? Not for a loved one who has been given release from pain. We are sorry for ourselves. Our pattern of living has been upset. We are forced to find a new focus for our attention, a new interest for life. This is the tragedy of the family that has lived for itself alone.

In contrast, there is the story of a brilliant young man who played in a symphony orchestra. Night after night, in one of the front seats sat his aged father. Although he had lost years ago his faculty of hearing, the father still was enjoying in memory the music he could no longer hear. One night the front seat was vacant. A fellow musician, attempting to express his sympathy at the young man's loss of his father, said, "It's too bad your father couldn't have heard the symphony tonight." The young man responded, "You are wrong, my friend. Tonight for the first time in many years my father

heard the symphony." Here was a faith and an interest great
enough to reach into eternal life. What a blessing have they
who have taken God into the partnership of their lives, and
permitted their earthly love to be welded with an everlasting
union.

It was of such that our Lord spoke when He said:
"Blessed are they that mourn for they shall be comforted."
They shall behold through the eyes of God the valley of
vision.

God could have used some other means of completing
the transition from this life to the next. The fact remains
that He did not. He, whose purpose for us is that we shall
inherit the best and win eternal life, has known always what
some of us are beginning to discover—that nothing in life
that is worthwhile comes to us without some effort and some
cost. Whatever purpose is served through sorrow, it is not
that we shall be injured or punished, but that through it, we
may rise stronger to meet the tests of life.

The prophet Micah has given us a significant picture of
this. He describes a silver refiner sitting cross-legged before
his charcoal fire. Suspended above it on a tripod is the metal
container of bubbling, steaming silver ore. When this ugly
mass is exposed to the heat, the impurities are removed. Time
and again the refiner peers into the vessel. He is waiting for
the moment when his image is perfectly reflected in the
metal. Then he knows it is pure and ready for use. Perhaps,
in a similar way, God peers into the crucible of our lives
where the worthless and the cheap are being consumed by
the fire of pain and hardship. He is looking for the pure
metal of a man in order that when he finds it, he may use it
for his more glorious work. Here is a clue to the purpose of
some of our sorrow.

A great teacher of religion has stated it thus: "Whether
an event shall bless or curse us is determined not by the

vent, but by the character of the response which we make
o it."

James Weldon Johnson has given us in Negro dialect
he call of faith as he experienced it in his own life. From
is valley of vision he pictures for us God's way of looking at
leath and the life to come.

Weep not, weep not,
She is not 'dead,'
She's resting in the bosom of Jesus.
Heart-broken husband—weep no more;
Grief-stricken son—weep no more;
Left-lonesome daughter—weep no more;
She's only just gone home.

Day before yesterday morning,
God was looking down from his great, high heaven,
Looking down on all his children,
And his eye fell on Sister Caroline,
Tossing on her bed of pain.
And God's big heart was touched with pity,
With the everlasting pity . . .

And God said: 'Go down, death, go down,
Go down to Savannah, Georgia,
Down in Hamacraw
And find Sister Caroline.
She's borne the burden and the heat of the day,
She's labored long in my vineyard,
And she's tired—
She's weary—
Go down, death, and bring her to me.'

While we were watching round her bed,
She turned her eyes and looked away,

She saw what we couldn't see:
She saw old death. She saw old death,
Coming like a falling star.
But death didn't frighten Sister Caroline;
He looked to her like a welcome friend.
And she whispered to us: 'I'm going home,'
And she smiled and closed her eyes . . .

This simple confidence expressed in the imagery of
plain people tells us of the character of the response a be
lieving man can make to the great unknown.

If you have love, sorrow lies inescapably ahead. Com
to grips with this fact now. God can turn your valley of dark
ness into vision. He summons you to bring that vision t
others. We know we shall one day come face to face wit
loss. Now is the time to take a "view from the ridge"—to see
and find the assurance which will enable us to stand in tha
uncertain day. Do not wait until you are forced to grope as
child in the valley. But turn like a man to Christ, whose fee
have spanned all the valleys of life, and find through Hir
your "valley of vision."

Father, Son, and Spirit

*

CHARLES, wilt thou have this woman to thy wedded wife . . .
nd forsaking all others, keep thee only unto her so long as
e both shall live?"

The father of the groom stood in the family pew beside
is wife and watched the ceremony with mingled feelings.
Ie was glad that the love of his son, latent during the first
ears of manhood, had found an object so worthy as Alice.
But there was the other feeling—that of loss.

". . . Forsaking all others . . ." certainly this meant par-
nts. He glanced to his right. The look on Mary's face told
im she was feeling it, too. There was a finality about this
eparation. It had been coming for the past seven years. The
oretaste of it they had experienced the day Charles, with
he flush of excitement on his face, boarded the plane for
ollege, leaving behind him an empty room. After college
ad come three years in the Air Force. Meanwhile the family
ad moved to Cleveland. No need of a boy's room in the new
ouse. Chuck could use the guest room when he returned on
eave. Yet somehow he was always "coming home"—still a
art of the household—until now.

"I, Alice, take thee, Charles, to my wedded husband;
o have and to hold from this day forward . . ." Who, having
aid these words, does not recall his own expression of them

whenever he hears them repeated? But this time it is a new
vow. The old was left behind at the chancel step.

Bride and groom kneel before the altar for the Church's
blessing upon their pledge each to the other. There is a hush.
Then the great organ announces to the world the joy that is
written on their faces. Chapter I of the drama *A Man and a
Woman and God* has begun for Charles and Alice.

On the way home from the reception Charles Sr. broke
the silence. "If any more people had said to me, 'You're not
losing a son; you're gaining a daughter,' I think I'd have
flipped."

"Well, we did," countered Mary.

"Did what?"

"Gained a daughter."

With a degree of firmness, Charles replied, "All right,
think this if you want to—and I'm glad you feel that way—
but hands off! They're not children; they're adults, married
and everything. Remember what the Bible says: "For this
cause shall a man leave father and mother and cleave to his
wife." Mary smiled, "All right, professor—or should I say
padre?"

How right they are! The new family must be free to
assume its responsibilities, to make decisions, to take the
initiative—free of interference from in-laws especially. And
why not? If the two homes from which Charles and Alice
came have done their respective parts, the new home will
unconsciously incorporate in itself the best of the old—
values, standards, customs, expressions, attitudes, even taste
for food, traditions, and pastimes. What is more, two families
will stand by, ready to advise and assist when needed. In the
weeks to come Alice will call her mother for information
about everything from babies to biscuits. Chuck will likewise
be asking and receiving advice from Dad. This is the function of "in-laws"—to stand by with power to help, but unless
that help is sought and wanted, to get out of the way.

Mary awakened the following morning to the clatter of pans downstairs, accompanied by mumbled expressions of a male voice. "Oh that man," she grumbled, "a day off, and he has to disturb the household—and at this hour!" What hour was it? She looked at her wristwatch—ten o'clock. Quickly, apology ready, she descended to the kitchen, where, presumably, breakfast was in process. None was in sight. Not even coffee perking. Down one more flight of stairs she found the cause of the cacaphony that had interrupted her sleep. There in the recreation room was Charles, gruntingly retrieving a dozen or so small reels of film in tin cases, from the floor.

"Did you have to make all that racket?"

"Well, you wanted these shelves cleared. Just be thankful these things aren't made of glass." Mary assisting in the recovery, noted some of the labels: Wedding '36; Yellowstone '38; Cottage '40; Fort Benning '42; Summer '46! Christmas '44. They brought back memories.

Charles too was daydreaming. He thought of their own wedding day, so much like yesterday—clear October sky, autumn leaves in full color, the fragrance of apples in the countryside. Honeymoon days—new love sacramentally expressed; trout over an open fire. Down-to-earth days—the first apartment; the first promotion; the first anniversary; the first baby!

It was the day of the Baptism. Charles and Mary really began to feel as if they were a part of St. George's Church. For several months they had been regular attendants. What started them? Was it the friends they had met at the couples club—or was it the desire to know more about God, who was soon to bless their home with a gift of a child?

Now the gift was theirs—a blond bundle of masculine energy. Chapter II had begun for them. These were the "how-to" days: how to bathe, feed, change; how to insert pablum in a twisting, turning face; how to sleep between feedings; how to contain one's pride in the presence of visitors. Looking ahead—how to be better parents than some you read about in the papers; how to give this boy what he needs to grow physically strong, mentally keen, morally sound; how to guide this life toward the fulfillment of the purpose for which God designed it. This is a job that calls for more than parents can muster from their own resources. Granted! Charles and Mary sought the help of a pediatrician —learned about child care, nutrition, and preventive medicine. Correspondingly, they were beginning to think of their son's intellectual growth. A portion of income was already earmarked for education. Now, at this moment of the Baptism they were seeking Divine help and guidance in order to discharge in a third area their stewardship of this life entrusted to them. Together they prayed, "Give thy Holy Spirit to this child that he may be born again and made an heir of everlasting salvation . . ."

"Born again!" For the first time in his life these words came alive for Charles. Were they not, as parents, witnessing to three kinds of life in this child of theirs? Physical birth is a biological act—the severing of a cord and a cry—he lives! Not long afterward this same baby came alive mentally. He soon learned how to use his capacity to cry to accomplish his own ends. He had no sooner been brought home than he tried out his secret weapon. At the first burst from his lungs and vocal cords, inexperienced adults came running. Anxious hands quickly discovered the cause of the noise. Soon infant was warm and dry where he had been cold and wet. Silence reigned. A few hours later the same baby effort produced the same result. This time exploring parents finding no need of clothing change, arrived at the other conclusion— warmed a bottle, and gave nourishment. Thus the first step in the learning process was accomplished. From that moment on, tiny Charles knew he had but to cry to bring one or both grown people to his side. Thus he "came alive" mentally. He was born anew into the realm of thought, decision and knowledge.

Soon there came a new quality to this knowledge. The infant was to discover that the hands which attended him were tender, loving hands. The voice that spoke to him was soft and soothing. Eventually such treatment was to bring forth from him a smile or a coo—the first human response to love. Here was a third "birth" about to take place—an awakening to the world of the spirit. In a human sense and in a very small way this child was being "born again." The great awakening that must come to life in order for it to have meaning is the Spiritual birth (with a capital S). One must "come alive" unto God—must come to recognize that God is Love and life, and learn to live on the basis of this recognition. We are body, mind, and spirit. Medicine with all of its discoveries stands ready to serve our physical needs. We are keenly aware of this. We depend heavily upon this knowledge and skill. Wisely so. Education in home and school will serve to develop our mental processes and satisfy our intellectual needs. A great portion of time and life must be devoted to this second accomplishment. But how many there are whose awareness of need never goes beyond these two levels. Neither they nor their children come alive spiritually. So they miss completely the "reason why." Motives remain dwarfed by material values. Relationships continue to be "infantile" and self-centered. The capacity for selfless love goes undeveloped. Hope is limited to what can be achieved by brawn and brain. Faith never has a chance. Man spends his life seeking the answer to the question, "Who am I?" In doing so, he misses asking the far more important question, "Whose am I?"

Charles and Mary have, in their short year of marriage, come alive spiritually. Friendships, pastimes, values, goals, have been shaped according to a new dimension. They have gone in search of the answer to the question "Why?" They found that the Church gave them clues. They had never enjoyed anything so much as their relationship with other young families they met through St. George's, people like themselves, who were in quest for the deeper meaning of life. Some of the group, like themselves tired of the treadmill of life—eat-sleep-work-eat-sleep-work—invited them to a study course on "What does it really mean to be a Christian?" It took some time to brush away the cobwebs of their own ignorance; a little longer to discover the real meaning behind some of the Bible stories they half remembered from child-hood. Then a whole new world of thought and considera-tion came to be theirs. Religion for the Christian doesn't mean merely good thoughts and good deeds, and following rules. It isn't based on "blind faith." Neither is it founded on fear; nor is it nourished on superstition.

Christianity starts where many people stop thinking: "In the beginning, God." It isn't enough merely to accept the thought of a purpose or power behind the world which "some people call God." What is really important is to find out what kind of a God is at the heart of things and how much He offers even now to those who will choose to live their lives according to His design. Christians believe in a God who "so loved the world that He gave His only begotten Son"—"Who for us men and for our salvation came down from heaven." He is not an aloof God, but a God who cares and is personally interested in each of us. How childish it now seemed to Charles and Mary to have tried to operate their lives spiritually on their own resources alone. They were beginning to understand that a part of the Divine Plan was for humans to draw on the great source of help and strength that God makes available to us. To be a Christian means to stake your life on the fact that God is, as Christ illustrated Him to be. He's not just a "First Cause" who left us with a set of rules. He is like a father—indeed He is related to all men and to each of them as Charles is, in his heart, related to his little son. God is the source of life and of the Help and Strength we can never deserve, but for which we may ask and which we may receive. One takes for granted that such "gifts" as love, joy, peace, forgiveness, humility, kindness, are human achievements. On the contrary, they are the fruits of life that is "alive unto God," drawing its nourishment from Him. Charles and Mary want this quality of life for themselves in their own relationship. They want it even more for their son. Therefore they have brought him to Baptism, offering themselves together with their sponsors, to be the spiritual family through whom God shall work. In this service they express their confidence that He will accept this moment as the point of beginning, a new birth into life, the goal of which is unity with the heavenly Father—"that he (Charles) may be born again (into the life of the Spirit) and be *made* an heir of everlasting salvation."

Charles and his son brought their outboard to shore just as the first great drops of rain began to pelt them from the threatening cloud overhead. Amazing what a six-year-old can accomplish in an hour with a little patient coaching. This was their first fishing trip together. Son and father were becoming reacquainted. The nightmare of the war years was over. The infrequent letters bearing their picture—story of Chuck from infancy to boyhood—all this was forgotten in the present opportunity to become a family once again. So, vacation had brought three, instead of the former two, to the little lakeside cabin. Charles, the boy, learned quickly from his stranger-father how to bait and how to troll without getting the line in the motor. Then there was the first "strike"—the bending rod, the cranking reel, and finally the first sight of a bass breaking water. Now the words of the "coach" came with rapidity: "Let him run; play him; reel him in; let him go." After a five-minute "hour" the catch was brought into the boat. Mary could hear from the shore above the chug of the little motor the shrill "I caught him! Gee, Dad." How she had longed for this during the months of separation when she had tried to be both father and mother.

The older fisherman was not so absorbed in his sport that he failed to notice the rising cloudbank in the west. He knew when it was time to "head for shore." They just made it. Now safely sheltered in the cottage, they awaited the fury of the summer shower. It came with a blazing flash of lightning, followed by a deafening crash of thunder. The little boy searched with anxious eyes the face of his father, ready to react in terms of the expression he saw there. Fortunately, the reaction was a good one. "Bang," said the father. "Firecrackers" said the boy. Then both of them laughed. In a matter of seconds an attitude was established that was to be lifelong. How easily this experience might have filled this child with terror, if the father's reaction had been one of alarm! Treated with calm acceptance, father revealed to son the way a man meets a storm—with caution, but unafraid. Such an experience was worth ten thousand words of explanation.

Whether we want to be or not, to our children we are the way, the truth, and the life. The question is what "way" shall our lives lead them? Shall they see the truth through us? They look to us often at unexpected moments. What we register in attitude, expression, and reaction will indelibly stamp their personalities. So does a child experience love or hate, fear or courage, wisdom or foolishness, childishness or maturity, superstition or trust. Here, in a vacation moment, we see a family living Chapter II, the interpretive chapter of the drama *A Man and a Woman and God*.

To create, as at birth, is one complete and separate function. A child, so soon as he is delivered, might be placed in a foster home and raised by quite another family. One work is finished. Yet the moment creation is accomplished, a family must turn to its second great function—that of revelation. Parents must make known to the child entrusted to them—either by the miracle of birth or by adoption—the meaning and significance of life. As we have noted, the greatest instrument of communication is not what parents say, but what they are, day by day and hour by hour. It is evident that they shall fail utterly to impart worthy concepts to their children unless for them as adults life has meaning and purpose. So there rests upon them life's most gigantic responsibility. Every moment of every day, each experience of life is a learning situation. Parent is both teacher and illustration. Family life is the laboratory in which the elements of character are explored, tested, proved, and used. Here primarily is the combination "drawing board, shop, and testing ground" for all human equipment. Here facts take form. Words become flesh. Ideals become acts. Values are incorporated in experience and judgment. Home is both the cradle and the school of freedom, democracy, love, forgiveness, understanding, faith, and religion. What the family is, its offspring are likely to be also.

Charles and Mary, now grandparents, have reflected often upon life's three great chapters: the Creative, the Interpretive, the Supportive. They see each one as an inseparable part of the other two. A family creates; it makes known; it stands by with power to help. Little wonder that for them the Church's doctrine of the Holy Trinity should be so meaningful. They too have been a trinity, in the image of God.

They believe:

In "God the Father (who creates), maker of heaven and earth,"

And in Jesus Christ (who makes God known), "the Way, the Truth, and the Life,"

In God the Holy Spirit, the Dynamic, ever-present, empowering God, who stands by, awaiting our wanting Him, to uplift, support, and sanctify these lives of ours.

This great truth was there all the time, awaiting their understanding of it.

As they stand facing the cross on a Sunday morning, they say the Creed as their oath of allegiance, as their pledge of loyalty, as their act of rededication. While they only "know in part" the great truths the Creed contains, they recognize it as the Faith of the Church. Through their own participation in the life, worship, and teaching of the Church, more and more that creed has become their own. They are living it every day.

PART II

The Family Rediscovers Religion

Houses

SEE THEM stretching out there into the distance, row upon row for miles: little houses, big houses, square ones, oblong ones, high-reaching apartment buildings. Together they spell "City, U.S.A." Houses may look different on the outside, but what really makes them different is what we find within. Perhaps if we were to visit one or two of them, we would see how very different they actually are. One is a symphony of color and beauty inside. Another is drab and forbidding. One is a home enjoyed by those who live there. Another is just a house—a place in which the occupants eat and sleep, from which they hurry away for the day or for the evening.

Our real interest is in people. In a way, they are like their houses. They look somewhat alike. They wear similar clothes, drive similar cars. Most of them have had, or will have, quite similar experiences. It is the way they live and the way they meet these experiences that makes them different. Here, for example are husband and wife, just starting life together. Perhaps in another home there are tired children, full of the events of the day. Dinner is over. The little ones are scurrying from person to person bestowing their ceremonial good night kisses, and postponing "bed" as long as possible. Perhaps there are young people who have put aside their school books. No studies tonight! Just *try* to use that telephone until their plans for the evening are completed! Or it may be that we are seeing an older couple who remember these experiences from other days. Grandfather is reading the paper. Grandmother still lingers over the dinner dishes. Presently she'll join him and together they'll enjoy their favorite television program. Young or old, these families look very much alike to you and me. Here's the great difference. Some of them are happy, some unhappy. Why is this? It's not the way we appear to be. It's what we believe and what we do about it that makes us different. It's the way we live, the fun we have, the friends we make, the dreams we fashion—it's what we want from life that makes us different. It's the rule of life we follow, the values we cherish—the motives that possess us and the convictions we hold—that determine whether life will yield for us a measure of happiness, or whether every flame of experience will end in the ashes of bitterness.

The family story—yours and mine—is often like the hearth fires we lay. A few pieces of dry kindling will flare brilliantly for an instant, leaving cold, dark ashes in a moment. Dissatisfaction with this type of fuel has caused man to dig deep into the earth for more durable fuel, the warmth and glow of which will give lasting comfort and enjoyment.

We who would find happiness that is durable must dig deep into the reasons for living. We may choose if we wish the quick thrill of a moment of self-satisfaction. But be prepared for the "ashes." On the other hand, we may seek the deeper joy that comes of making others happy.

I have known quarrelsome homes that shattered and disintegrated because they were fashioned of the kindling of selfish demands and childish, petty grievances. I have known homes that have weathered every storm of failure and sorrow, have breasted every wave of success and joy, because the family "fuel" for life was unselfish love which overcame all personal differences.

Kahlil Gibran in his little book *The Prophet* places the question squarely before us. This is what he says:

"Tell me—what have you in these houses? What is it you guard with fastened doors? Have you peace, the quiet urge that reveals your power? Have you remembrances, the glimmering arches that span the summits of the mind? Have you beauty that leads the heart from things fashioned of wood and stone, to the holy mountain? Tell me, have you *these* in your houses? Or have you only comfort and the lust for comfort, that stealthy thing that enters the home a guest and then becomes a host and then a master?"

What have you in your house? What kind of a family story are you writing? Now it would be easy to dismiss this question if it were merely your home or mine that was at stake. But a far greater responsibility rests upon us. John Ruskin once said that the Roman Empire fell because the family system decayed. History has proved again and again how right he was. The strength of America, the very life of democracy, depends upon these homes of ours.

Out of them shall come tomorrow's citizens. Some will be arrogant rebels, who know no law, except to "take what they can get!" They know no loyalty except to themselves. They know no love except the craving for satisfaction. They have no sense of responsibility; no desire to serve; no concept of anything greater than they. Theirs were very likely broken homes, unhappy homes, mere "kindling" homes, where life was soon reduced to ashes.

Out of other homes shall come citizens whose characters are tempered by affection and understanding. They know what it means to share, for the best of life has been shared with them. They are equipped to lead, because they have learned to follow. They have the capacity to understand because their home was a laboratory of human relationships. They know loyalty because they have learned respect. They are capable of mercy because they have experienced forgiveness. They have learned that lasting happiness is a treasure of the heart, not of the bank account. Whether from cottage or mansion, they are able to meet the storm, as well as the calm, of life with courage and vision. They have dug deep for the meaning of life. They have found it and incorporated it in their home and family. Upon such as these, the future of our country depends.

Is there some particular ingredient which helps one family do its job while another fails? I believe there is. Kagawa, that great Japanese Christian once said this about it: "There can be no attainment of sacred love, nor can the perfecting of home life be hoped for, without religious faith." That sounds easy. All we have to do is to believe that there is some kind of a god and, presto, our lives are happy.

We know it isn't as simple as this. Religion is the act of God touching our lives, and our response to him. It is knowing God and as the result of that knowledge, understanding ourselves and what it is He wants us to do. Until we begin to do this, religion will be of very little help or meaning to us. God has always offered us this knowledge. But our little minds have often failed to grasp the truth, or our wills have rejected it. Do you remember the days when the radio was a crystal set with earphones? How we struggled to adjust that little device to the broadcast! At last if we were very patient, we might catch a few notes of a symphony. Then in a burst of static, it faded away. It may have been glorious music, but those little radios were not equipped to receive it. So God, whose character is Love, and whose purpose is our true happiness, has sought to reach us, but the static of our minds —fear, ignorance, pride, or immaturity—has stood in the way. One day, knowing our difficulty, God entered history. God provided us with the best receiving set of all—human experience. "God so loved the world that He gave His Son, Jesus Christ." For the first time, our world saw God in terms of human understanding. As a result, we have seen the purpose of God, more significant than His power. Now we may come to know that God loves us with a greater love than any earthly father ever loved his son. He seeks our love in return.

We are in a position to grasp the meaning of an old rule: "Thou shalt love the Lord Thy God with all thy heart and with all thy soul and with all thy mind and with all thy strength." We may discover, too, what in God's eyes it means to be a man: "Thou shalt love thy neighbor as thyself"— that is, as thou art loved by God. This is the foundation that will bring happiness to the families who build their lives upon it.

Love for Christians is far more than sentiment or infatuation. It is more than the endowment of one's mate with worldly goods. Christian love means that man and wife, in their relationships, mirror the Divine Love: each wants with all his heart to see the other supremely happy, wants it enough to take the necessary steps to make it so. Sometimes I picture family life as a great triangle. At the base of it we find the man and the woman. Something greater than either of them must draw these two people together at a pinnacle of thought and concern for each other. For a time, children may draw their interest upward, beyond themselves. But the children are soon grown up. Before we fully realize it, the peak of the triangle is gone. Sometimes this bond of common interest and unselfish concern may be a vacation or a new home or a favorite pastime. Each in its turn loses its drawing power, leaving nothing in its place but emptiness. There is only one permanent apex for our triangle which will last a lifetime. That is God, as we are drawn to love and serve Him. Now we have the Eternal Triangle as it should be. Here is the framework for real happiness. A man and a woman and God.

If we wish to build a house to stand a lifetime, we choose an experienced architect to make the plan. We seek a reliable builder who will follow the blueprint. We use great care in selecting our materials. We make sure the foundation is strong. We ascertain that the plan is structurally sound. Then we build with confidence. God is the Great Architect of homes that will last. But He is more than a Designer. He helps us build for, you see, He hopes soon to be invited there as a Guest.

Family life according to the Eternal Plan means we must choose with care the human materials—the qualities of character with which we build. Look into your own personality for honesty, respect, purpose, understanding, unselfishness, loyalty, forgiveness, faith. It is out of these materials that love is fashioned.

Recognize children as a trust from God. Know life itself to be a gift from God. We shall need His help every step of the way if our home is to be what God intended it to be. If our family story is to be long and full of happiness, build on the sure foundation of faith in the heavenly Father, made known to us through Christ.

Have you found the happiness of a home that is built on spiritual foundations? If you have, then your family story is worth reading. It is a story of a home that is built on the solid rock of belief that God is the true Head of every family. You have responded with heart and mind and will to this conviction. Your story may not make the headlines. But be assured that many families will read what your life has written. They will take courage from it. Some will see by contrast the cause of the void in their own lives and take steps to correct it. The eager young eyes of those who dream of the day when they will take the leap of faith into family life will take hope from your story and seek and find the surer way to their own happiness. You can make no greater contribution to the future of our country, no nobler response to God's plan, than to build and sustain a family whose story is written in the indelible letters of love and faith.

Growth

THIS IS the story of two boys, Jim and Joe, who claimed a man's privileges, but who as boys were unable to make use of them. Let us look first at Jim's situation. Jim and his parents share the typical life of many families in a small American community. Jim is fourteen and large for his age; he will begin high school next fall. Right now he has a paper route and rides a bicycle. He is interested in cars and mechanics. "All this education stuff is the bunk," he says. "What a fellow really needs is a job." He tried to talk to Dad about it last week, but he didn't get anywhere. "You're too young, son; wait a few years until you're really ready to tackle the world." "Yea, wait a few years . . . Be a good boy; go to school; go to Sunday school . . . and then the army will get you. Not for me. I'm going to have some fun. I'm going on my own."

It was "kind of hard" drawing his savings; harder still to leave the note for Mom. But she'll understand, he thought.

Jim had to find out the painful way. The last six weeks have not been easy. He landed a job right away. It was easy in the city, where no one knows you, to pass for 18. But with no experience, he had had to take a low-paying job and wait his turn to apprentice. He misses home and his own room. No one to talk to. He misses mother's apple pies and home cooking. He misses the gang that used to play touch football together, and then raid the ice box and watch television. He knows no one except the men in the shop who hurry home after work. Oh yes, he knows the landlady. She wants her rent money in advance. What to do?

See what his rebellion has cost this boy! He has forfeited all the grace of family life. He has lost companionship and the blessings of love. He has lost prestige and reputation, and forfeited his sense of belonging, of being wanted. He has deprived himself of the mature wisdom and judgment of his parents. He has lost the opportunity of preparing for life step by step, using his own home as the proving ground for his thoughts and actions and opinions. He has cut himself loose from the roots of "life with a meaning and a purpose." Now he clutches the faded and withering blossom of freedom which is no freedom at all. All of this he has denied himself simply because he wanted to do what he wished when he wanted to do it.

Joe, on the other hand, is a student at Brighton College. However, he is about to cut himself off from his heavenly Father, and from the Family of God. He imagines that he has found a conflict between science and religion. Like most young men in his predicament, he doesn't know much about either. His introduction to biology started him thinking about how life developed. Then came Psychology I, with its suggestion of the importance of the mind and of the "illusion" called religion. To climax it all, two of the boys in the philosophy course were saying it was just old fashioned to accept blind faith in God when there are so many "facts" you can depend upon. A few of the really "smart" students he knows are skeptics—"I'm from Missouri; you have to show me." Joe thinks this makes good sense to him. He used to believe in God and religion, but there's so much to learn and there are so many who know more than he does . . . he . . . well . . . he just doesn't know. Some folks would tend to blame the college or the university for upsetting this boy's faith. I don't think so. The real root of the problem goes back to Joe's boyhood and to the kind of world in which he was living. In 1941 Dad had been called into service. During the war, mother tried to do her patriotic duty. She worked days as a volunteer in First Aid, and at night, the swing shift at the defense plant. When Sunday came, she was so tired she slept all morning. Joe didn't always get to Sunday school. When he did get there, they were always talking about peace and about loving your neighbors. When he got home, everybody was talking about the war and about how many enemy planes had been shot down. The Church and war just didn't seem to go together. The Sunday school teacher used to read to them about Adam and Eve, and about David and the giant, and about the Baby Jesus. When Joe was thirteen he felt too old to go to Sunday school. When dad returned home, he and mother spent Sundays, fishing or playing golf. Church couldn't be so important, or else Dad would be going, too. Dad was a hero. His mother told him so, and she had his oak leaf cluster to prove it.

Now, in college, Joe just can't seem to make much sense out of religion. Small wonder. What has he to depend upon? A weak thread of Sunday school stories he only half remembers. A children's custom that was not even supported by the adults nearest him. What child's toy will ever serve a man? Here at school are grown-up studies for adult minds. But there are no courses in religion or in the Bible. (Some people are worried about Church and State or something.) Think of it—a few scattered bits of childhood knowledge about the Bible and religion! How could they possibly dovetail into education on the college level? How proud the instructor must be who can shatter this flimsy foundation! What an achievement to commit religious infanticide! Joe has been let down by society, by his family, by his Church, by the century, and now he is to be robbed of the motive power of his life. What good is knowledge without the motive to use it constructively? It takes a man whose life has a spiritual foundation to live nobly and to assist others to do the same. Knowledge is essential, but the will to use it for good is even more essential.

Joe has about decided to leave God out of his future. He's going to go it alone. Two attitudes toward life are possible for him.

He may suppose that he is like a tiny, helpless piece of driftwood on a mighty and relentless sea. Everything that he is or will be is determined by forces that are beyond his control. His ancestors have shaped his life; or he is the product of the chemistry of his own body. He is like a puppet drawn up or down by the strings of history. He is the helpless pawn of the state. Then again, it may be "fate" or the "stars" that have set the course of his life and determined his personality. It would be very convenient if this were all there were to life. There would be no responsibilities whatever for a man. In fact there would be no reason whatever to go on living. The fact that we *do* have power to alter history and to change the course of our own lives spells the lie to this kind of reasoning. It takes religion to make us aware of these responsibilities.

The second possible attitude for one who chooses to live without God is the exact opposite of the first. Man is all that matters. Whatever is to be done, he must do.

There is a story about two boys which tells how each of them at one time found his rowboat firmly stuck in a sandbar at low water mark. One of them got out of the boat and began to dig with his hands to free the vessel. The other said, "Let's wait for the return of the tide." The viewpoint that man is all may be likened to the boy digging with his hands in the sand. The man with religion is in one way like the boy who waits for the tide. For without God there can be no Saviour; man must save himself. But what can one man do against the great forces around him? This pathetic person suddenly discovers the tremendous need to become strong. He must find someone to help him, for two are stronger than one. But the two discover they must find a third, and the three a fourth, and so on, until the group becomes a gang bent on saving itself, and the gang becomes a mob. But still, they cannot wrest from life the benefits they want. So they decide that someone must be to blame. They look for a scapegoat—an individual, or a group, or a race—to put the blame on. The accused finds it necessary to protect himself. By the same process, he too must become strong. Eventually two rival forces are created out of fear. The fear ripens into hate; the hate explodes in destruction. Who suffers? The proud little man who was going to save himself. If it happens between communities, we have prejudice and tyranny and misery; and no one is safe. If it happens between nations, we have war.

The person who cuts himself off from God has another problem. He dismisses his authorities. He no longer has any reason for reaching toward the best that he can do with his life. The only standard of values he now has must be borrowed from the group or the civilization to which he belongs. If he wants to be content with his lot, he simply looks for someone who is doing a poorer job than he.

The godless man in America borrows his standard of values from his neighbors. Or he borrows his standard of citizenship from the past—from men whose honesty, vision, faith, and respect for human life are deeply rooted in religious conviction. This unbeliever is fortunate. Even a parasite can live well if it feeds on a strong body. But suppose another generation comes which scorns honesty and perverts truth. Suppose it should become fashionable to stamp out the weak, to destroy or enslave men. What then would our spiritual stowaway use as a standard by which to live and to measure the value of human life? "Man is all or man is nothing." One of these attitudes toward life will belong to Joe who tossed out his religion. Both of them will end in disappointment and defeat. If only this lad in our story could know that real religious knowledge and the knowledge of science and philosophy are not in conflict at all. They complement one another. It takes some fresh and factual knowledge in each field to enable one to discover this is so.

Once a year you and your family go shopping somewhere for a Christmas tree. You select one of the saplings from the display and bring it home to brighten your home during the holidays. Perhaps the whole family together will trim it with strings of light, festoons of popcorn, dazzling ornaments, and tinsel icicles. It will stand in the corner of your living room as a symbol of Yuletide and of your expectation of the return of spring when the trees will be green once more. But not this tree. Within a few days its needles will fall. The dry branches will drop under the baubles. Having served its brief purpose, it will be stripped of its ornaments and discarded. God had another plan for that little tree. He planned it to grace the forest as a tall and stately pine, to hold moisture in the earth, to give shade and shelter to man and beast. Finally, it might have been taken in its glorious maturity to serve a lasting purpose—as lumber for a home to stand for a century, or as the foundation for a book whose message might bring light to seeking minds for generations. Such was its destiny. But man interfered—cut it loose from its roots, condemned it to be an ornament sold for a few dollars and then cast away.

In God's plan, neither trees nor men will fulfill their destinies unless provision is made for them to reach maturity. Moral and spiritual values will live and grow and develop in us *only* as long as they are rooted and grounded in the good soil of faith in God.

The two boys chose to live their lives separated from

their roots: Jim from his earthly father; Joe from his heavenly Father. Both must take the consequence, each in his own way. Each has denied himself the grace that could have given him maturity and the help to fulfill his destiny as a man. But because they could not see that real freedom is in discipline, not in rebellion, they lost the opportunity to be really free.

There is a Bible story about all the Jims and Joes of this world. It is the story of the Prodigal Son. (Luke 15:11) It is the story of a boy who wanted to "go it alone," had his chance, and failed. So God the Father grants us our childish desire to "go it alone," hoping and praying that very soon, we will come to ourselves, be done with the hell and the husks of life, and return to Him. As in the story, God the Father will not force upon us His way of life. He loves us too much to take away our freedom. He will wait until we want the kind of life He planned for us—want it enough to come to Him and ask Him for it.

Studdert Kennedy has pictured the Jims and Joes to be like the sailor who went off as a boy to sail the seas and never returned. But every night in his father's cottage a candle burned—a sign to the boy that he would be welcome at home.

As we press this figure a bit further, we may come to see that Christ is the beacon light to all mankind, telling us by what He is, through His Love and Forgiveness, that God is waiting—and will wait until the end of time if necessary—for you and me to return from our self-styled life and its futilities to be at-one with Him.

Through the Door

Today is odd jobs day for father—no office routine; no jangling telephone; no appointments! The inventories are over. The tax records are in. For the first time in many weeks his home is getting some attention. "Let's see—the back yard needs raking, and the fence repairing; replace a pane of glass in the garage door; wash and paint the porch floor; fix the front door." Somehow this last item had the most appeal. Chisel, plane, hammer, screwdriver, oil, and putty are assembled. Well-equipped, he stands before the door just as Jimmie rushes out to join his playmates. There, the cracks are filled, ready for painting. Let the spring rains beat upon it—inside, the family will be well-protected.

Father had not prepared, however, for the kind of storm that did come. Young Jimmie returned home, sobbing and with tears. He plunged through the door, piping his childish complaint to mother: "They wouldn't let me be pitcher, so I came home." By the time Jimmie was ready to venture forth again with new composure, Jack was bounding through the same door. "I'm hungry; what's there to eat?"

Meanwhile the door had been lifted clumsily from the hinges, the better to plane down its weather-swollen edges. Two screws needed replacement at the latch. Father remembered as a small boy how the one-way latch string at the old homestead was thrust through the little hole to permit friends and family to enter, and then drawn in at night for protection. This was a two-way latch. For the door must serve all who enter and all who leave the house. With some strain on his unused muscles, the door was lifted into place, only to come crashing down toward him as Bill emerged from the house.

As the older boy stopped to assist his father in the process of rehanging the repaired door, father learned that this was the "big day." Bill was on his way for an appointment about a summer job. Readjusting his tie, Bill started off for his date with "destiny."

The job was finally done. As father gathered his tools, he thought about the door and the drama he had just witnessed. Here was the connecting link between the individual and the outside world. This door was the means of refuge and refreshment. But it was also the exit into a world of opportunity and hope.

What this wooden entrance is to the old house, the family is to the persons who live in the house. It is the family that offers refuge and freshment for young and old, in order that they may go forth, strengthened to meet life. This family is the real door to the world. The attitudes, the insight, the principles of the parents will send those children forth with vision and values for life. Parents with a sense of humor seldom send a bore into life. The home that encourages honesty, that teaches courtesy and the social graces—the home that stimulates individual expression and sets an example in fairness and trust, is a door to confidence, to intelligent initiative, to democracy in action for the persons who pass through it.

I recall two families living in the same neighborhood with the same circle of friends, whose children attended the same school. The children of the one home were uncertain about their beliefs, selfish, spoiled, and negative toward life.

The children of the other family were full of confidence and optimism. They were sure of their beliefs, strong and mature, ready for life at its best, and able to face it at its worst. What made this difference was, of course, the family unit itself. One was a door of escape from reality and sent its children poorly equipped into life. It fed them on self-centeredness, indulgence and the thinnest broth of belief. The other was a door that entered upon nourishment and strength, sending its youth out to success and happiness.

What kind of a door to life does *your* home offer? Is your family a door to the life of responsibility and sharing, of love and self-sacrifice? Or is it a door that leads through indifferent arrogance into isolation, tyranny, superficiality, and sham?

Christians are familiar with still another use of the figure of the door. It was Jesus, the Nazarene, who said, "I am the door. . . . By me if any man enter, he shall be saved, and shall go in and out and find pasture." Do you recall how He first came to use that expression? It happened that day when the great Teacher and His students came upon a sheep stockade at sundown. Into this crude shelter the Palestinian shepherds led their little flocks to give them a place of rest and safety for the night. These men, who spent their lives upon the grass-covered hills protecting their flocks, became as life itself to the animals. With danger lurking in every woodland and valley, we can imagine that it was the practice of the shepherd to go ahead of the sheep, even into the sheepfold at night. So, one by one, these countrymen led their little flocks into the roofless barn. Here they stayed as one great flock until the morning. At dawn the sheep were divided again, when each shepherd, in turn, stood straddle-legged across the exit from the stockade, calling his own sheep. Only the animals accustomed to that voice would pass through the human door into the fields beyond. "And a stranger will they not follow, for they know not the voice of strangers" says the Scripture.

Now, Christ says to His disciples: "I am the door, the Way." I am the way to refreshment. "If any man thirst, let him come to me and drink"; and again, "I am the way" to life worth living. "Follow thou me." "I am the Door" to understanding. "Ye shall know the truth and the truth shall make you free." "I am the Door" to Everlasting Life. "No man cometh unto the Father but by me."

The Door—a connecting link between the man and his world. The Door—a two-way passage—inward to refreshment and strength; outward to life and happiness.

Christ is the Door to new strength. The Christian religion has frequently been regarded as a means of escape from life. Many have tried to use it as an escape from a past of which they are not proud, to provide a cloak of respectability for an unsatisfactory character. Some have hidden behind Bible verses to avoid facing the realities of life. But those who have brought their weaknesses honestly and sincerely and with repentance to Christ, have found in Him the way to overcome them. It is still true. Through Christ, the blind see; the deaf hear; the lame walk; the dumb speak; the hungry are fed. Those who are blind to the purpose of life—blinded by self-concern—are helped to see all humanity with a new sensitivity and tenderness. Those deaf to every voice except the cry of their own desires and plans, hear the great voice of God calling them to get out of their lonely rut and start listening for the joys and the needs of others. Those who limp along, stumbling over such obstacles as failure and self-pity, are bidden "rise up and walk" along the road of love and service for others. They who seek refuge in religion from the harshness of life *can* discover that the "hiding place" becomes an open field in which to work with courage. The crumb of bread they sought becomes a banquet. The moment of immunity for which they begged becomes permanent strength to withstand all the ravages of life. The little inoculation from fear and anxiety and worry which religion was supposed to give becomes a mighty transfusion that makes all life glow with new meaning and purpose, with new energy to reach up and take it.

A certain young lady of high intelligence and education began to find life increasingly meaningless and frustrating. Her excellent teaching position and good income offered her less and less of satisfaction. In a somewhat skeptical frame of mind, she turned to the Church, thus far untried and unexplored in her adult life. She found it a door to the refreshment of new reading and study. She made new friends. She developed new interests. She gained a new and healthier viewpoint through prayer. She established a new sense of direction for her energies in the Holy Communion. Today she is completely absorbed in a new life of service—at a smaller salary, but with a far greater income of peace and happiness. She would be the first to tell you that she has found Christ to be the Door that leads inward to strength, and outward to life worth living.

Christ is the Door to a new world of understanding and vision. Through this Door the man or the woman has a new sense of direction for his efforts. He has a sense not of seeking, but of being sought. The man in touch with Christ is like the aviator who pilots his ship across the night sky at "ceiling zero." His eyes are not on the earth, but on the instrument board before him. His ears are tuned to the control tower that is seeking him. All along he heard the beam signal. Now out of the baffling dark there comes the clear voice of the operator at the control tower summoning his flight for a landing. Down he plunges, out of the night, onto the landing field. While he has been seeking a landing, the man who is the way has been seeking him. So with life. For the Christian, someone with a more inclusive view is seeking him. God summons him to a clear landing on a field of worthier purpose. He has never been alone. Always the flight beam is there. His life was never designed for what he can get out of it, but that he shall "make the field" of God's purpose for him.

Christ is the Door to a new kind of opportunity—to the life that belongs not to man, but to God. His possessions are not his exclusively. They are his to bring happiness to others. His money is not his to own, but to share. His abilities are not his to abuse or to convert into cash; they belong also to his family and to his community and to his country. His time is not entirely his to invest in work and leisure; it is to be invested also in the development of his potentialities and his character. So there must be time for worship and refreshment and rest; for review and redirection to the truth that life is to *give* as well as it is to "get." He may follow some other plan of his own choosing. Indeed he is quite free to do so. But he will never find such happiness and peace as when he opens God's door of opportunity and walks through it to the "good pasturage."

Christ is the Door to that life which is continuous and eternal. The Christian religion deals with life, not with death. But it deals with the whole of life, not just a little earthly part of it. Through a doorway our family walks into the world. However much we parents may wish our children always to return home at nightfall, other interests, abilities, or duties may lead them to distant states and to other continents. When that happens, for the family a "big" world becomes small. Distance and time are no barriers where love is the bond of communication. Moreover, from childhood the home has equipped these young people for life out there.

Similarly, Christ and the Resurrection call us to see again the close connection God has made between our cottage-life of earth and the greater life that is to come. We, too, are called to look beyond our human threshold to the life that will one day be ours, provided daily life has equipped us with those abilities and qualities that are usable in the "life out there." The Christian knows that the vast "distance" between the "now" and eternity has been spanned by the Love of God. Therefore he tries to live today the kind of life that God can use forever. Christ is the Door to that life. He bids us, "Enter and be refreshed," and then, "Go forth and live."

Is It Really Love?

*

THERE IS unhappiness in the front room upstairs tonight.
Sister Sally came home early from work, her eyes tearstained.
No, she is not ill, just terribly unhappy. She has shut herself
in her room and refuses to eat—refuses to see anyone. She
lies on the bed, her body shaken with sobs. In all her nineteen years Sally has never acted nor felt like this. Mother
guessed the reason. She looked at her daughter's outstretched
left hand. The ring was missing from the third finger. Sally
had broken her engagement.

It was just two weeks ago that this same young lady had
come home late in the evening, her face radiant, starry-eyed,
fairly bursting with the news. She had danced into the living
room: "Dad, Mother, I have the most wonderful news. *I'm
going to be married!*" Sure enough, there on the third finger
of the left hand, was a small diamond. Nonetheless, this news
came as a great surprise to the family. Dad had asked, "Is it
Jack?" But little by little, the facts began to emerge. Jack
was at Fort Sand. He'd be coming home in a week or so,
before going overseas. Of course, it was the real thing. Yes,
she'd known him a "long time"—six months at least. Indeed,
Jack loved her; and she loved him.

Sally's parents were very wise. They knew the futility of
trying to combat heart with mind at this hour. They thought

she was too young; but they sensed the wave of feeling that sweeps many a young woman on toward marriage prematurely. Her mother remembered her own experience: the desire for companionship, the great hunger for home and family, the desire to be wanted, the feeling of maturity and independence that comes with job and income. Then there was the glamour of a man in uniform, and the man's need to feel he was a part of civilian life even though his plans for that life could only be hazy. The argument that others were doing it at nineteen. Perhaps, most compelling of all, there was the fear of being overlooked and forgotten.

These disturbed parents wished they had given some thought to how they might help their lovely daughter to grow up more leisurely. They might have helped her establish acquaintances. Perhaps if they had made their home a little more available—many thoughts crossed their minds, but all of them too late. Here was a young woman, with the direction of her life determined in her heart. They would give her as much encouragement, help, and understanding as possible. There were prayers that night that somehow this unknown youth, soon to be their son-in-law, would be the right man.

Now the engagement is over. Jack had come home on furlough. He had seemed to Sally not at all like a husband-to-be. He was full of small talk: "My experience; my plans; I want; I like; I think . . ." Sally wasn't so certain. Today she had seen him on the street with another girl. They'd had a talk later. "Well, perhaps it is better that we wait. See you sometime, Sally; write to me; here's my A.P.O. You're a peach to take it this way. Well, so long."

Tonight there were tears and shattered dreams. Too bad? (We're sorry for this girl's unhappiness). I think rather, how fortunate. There was nothing wrong with either of these two young people. They have simply discovered in time the truth—that they aren't in love. Sally's tears will dry. She doesn't think so tonight, but there will be other young men —and among them, the right one. What wonderful parents! No "I told-you-so's," but real understanding. A weekend in the country with Aunt Grace is just what Sally needs. And then, her job—and, perhaps, a course or two in the evening school. Wonder what that group of young adults at the Church are doing these days? Sally is taking it like a mature person.

For the average nineteen-year-old to make a good marriage is, in most cases, a happy accident. Marriage requires two persons deeply in love, equipped with real skill, and blessed with ideal circumstances to make that marriage a success.

No one wants to make a mistake about so important a matter as marriage. Life is not for experimentation. Most young persons would agree that they want to be sure about the life partner they choose. They want the real thing. Two questions arise: How can they be *sure*? and, Are they willing to take the necessary steps to make happy marriage a reasonable certainty? A man or woman will spend years in preparation for a life work. How many skilled physicians remember the long periods of rigorous training and self-discipline before they were ready to practice medicine! A great deal of their success is directly traceable to those lean years of hard work. Is it not also reasonable that life itself should have adequate preparation? Have we any right to expect a marriage to yield us a lifetime of happiness and satisfaction without real self-discipline, years of waiting, and thorough preparation?

I believe preparation for marriage is not a matter of weeks or months. It is a matter of years. "What? Do you mean to say that in this modern age a boy and girl should not consider marriage unless they have known each other for years?" I am much more concerned at this point that the boy know himself and that the girl know herself. Perhaps a few suggestions will help to explain what we mean.

Preparation for marriage might be thought of as consisting of four stages. Dr. Fritz Kunkel names these stages: Acquaintanceship, Friendship, Companionship, and Courtship. The first stage begins in the middle teens, and the last, somewhere in the early twenties. Preparation for marriage begins long before a certain boy meets a certain girl. Let us look at the first stage. Take Sally, for instance. There are those who remember when she was a shy, somewhat bookish girl of fifteen. How much she might have learned about her contemporaries, had she become better acquainted with the class at school. How many opportunities she overlooked for acquaintance—dramatics club, glee club, Hi-Y dances, school parties, church fellowships, her brother's friends. Here was a miniature city of young people she might have learned to know. Out of these hosts of people there would be those she disliked and there would be others who appealed to her. She would soon recognize the show-off. There might be others, like herself, suffering from shyness, ill at ease, not much to talk about. She would see herself as very much like some, and very different from others.

Had she gone through this experience, Sally now would be nearly ready for stage two: the Friendship stage. Out of that wide circle of people she knows, the smaller circle of friends begins to emerge. These friends have a schedule in which they get to know each other better—cokes at the sweet shop; recordings on Sunday; pizza parties, picnics, and corn roasts. A date now and then. How the group misses Mary, who now is "going steady." "Is this the fourth or fifth time?" Sally knows the playboys and the social butterflies. She begins to distinguish a tall tale from the truth. The Sunday study group on personality has helped her recognize the self-centered ones who are so boring, the complainers who haven't started to grow up, and the alibi-ikes who won't assume responsibilities.

Graduation week was one of the happiest in her life. A new chapter, in more than one way, has begun for Sally. The Third stage, the Companionship stage, is now in full bloom. Soon there will be separations, so the little group of friends are seeing a great deal of one another. There are long debates about work or college, marriage or a career.

But here the dream of "might-have-been" must end, for in point of fact the real Sally doesn't know enough about people or about herself to recognize at the outset that her affair with Jack is not really a love affair and can't last. Sally needs to remain for some time in the Companionship stage. There is plenty of time for courtship and marriage. This young lady needs to become thoroughly acquainted with some of her congenial associates. She needs new interests, new pastimes. She needs to establish in her mind the standards of behavior and character that her friends must meet. Life at home includes definite values and moral standards. Do her friends meet the test? If not, she'd better help them to achieve these standards, or be done with those as "friends" who consistently ridicule her belief and principles. She needs to ask herself why she likes this young man; what there is about another that doesn't ring true. What do her parents think about Bill or Joe or Grace or Jane?

If she learns these lessons, then one day it will happen. Sally will find herself at the fourth stage, the Courtship stage. Bob is becoming serious. Now all of her past experience must come to her aid. What does he have that the other boys do not have? How is he accepted by her friends? What do her parents think about him? Do they know she, too, is becoming seriously interested in Bob? Is this young man consistent in his behavior? Is he pretending to be the kind of person he thinks she will like? Or is this the real Bob? Has she been perfectly natural? Does he know her for what she is?

Now they are prepared to become engaged and to really talk it out. Have they an agreeing philosophy of life that is so necessary to happiness? What does he expect in a wife? What does she want in a husband? What is his attitude toward money? What are his plans for the future? Has he a job? Will it offer some opportunity for advancement? Has he a savings account? Has he thought about insurance? What kind of a home does he suggest? Will it fit into a budget on the income available? Does he believe his wife should be a breadwinner? Is he extravagant and lavish in his gifts? Can he afford to be? What does Bob think about a family? What type of people are his parents? Have they made a success of their marriage? Does he attend church? Are his beliefs in conflict with hers? What does he believe about God? Does he pray? Is he tolerant of others' views? Does he want to reach an agreement about religion? Must she give in to his viewpoint or, does he pass off differences with the comment that their love is the only thing that matters? What does he believe about marriage? Is it a legal contract? Or an economic agreement? Does he want to "give it a try," or does he speak of it as a *covenant* that is to last for life? Has he ever been married before? If he has, is there good reason to believe this new marriage will have a better chance of success?

There are myriads of questions, many of them complex. A qualified and reputable counselor or physician has a great deal to offer in helpful advice and information. Long before the date of the marriage is set, Sally and Bob should have consulted their clergyman. Here is a person deeply interested in their marriage, its permanence, its prospect for happiness. From the standpoint of his faith and profession, he is eager to explain more fully the spiritual implications in Christian marriage. He knows how many homes have been transformed by a living faith—how many tragedies have been overcome with the aid of the Grace of God. He has noticed that in many wrecked marriages religion has ceased to matter to one or both of the persons. He can tell of the many happy homes where marriage began and continued as a holy relationship —between a man and a woman and God. He knows that a marriage to have permanence must have heart and mind and will.

So Sally and Bob are to be married. How can they be sure that this is really love? They must continue to try to understand themselves in the weeks or months ahead. Dr. Fritz Kunkel, a noted psychologist, suggests this test for real love:

1. Has this relationship a sense of the "we," or do the man and woman still talk "I and me?" Is the "we" feeling mutual? Are they partners in a common cause?

2. Has their relationship the proper balance of physical and mental attraction?

When a gardener plants a fruit tree, he prunes it at intervals, cutting back the long slender shoots so they will branch out and grow in many directions, thus increasing the tree's capacity to bear fruit. If this romance has a one-stem basis—all physical or all intellectual, with no discipline or restraint, the partners have cheated themselves of many resources for happiness. If couples are really in love, they find they can enjoy themselves in innumerable ways.

3. Have they given themselves enough time?

4. How real is their knowledge of each other, and are they capable of evaluating it?

We said a moment ago that marriage is a spiritual venture. Like religion, it is based on faith. This does not mean, in either instance, a leap in the dark. It is rather, a step into the unknown of the future from the solid ground of experience, past and present. Sally and Bob know as much about each other as it is possible to discover before marriage. The next step requires more than mind and heart. It requires trust. On the basis of what they feel and know now, they are ready to face the future as man and wife, "forsaking all others." This is the faith that defies all uncertainties because it is based on the three great realities of marriage—a man, and a woman, and God.

So we pray for them and for all others who enter into family life, eager for happiness, and with love and faith.

O Perfect Love, all human thought transcending,
Lowly we kneel in prayer before Thy throne,
That theirs may be the love that knows no ending,
Whom Thou forevermore dost join in one.

Can You Stand Success?

A NEW FAMILY moved to Circleville this week. One morning a great yellow moving van arrived at the empty house on Elm Street. Father and Mother Rowe busied themselves arranging their familiar belongings in the unfamiliar rooms. Living room, dining room, kitchen—these were easily done. But the bedrooms were more of a problem. Sam would want this one with bookshelves for his library. That settles it. Harry must take the back room where his radios, trains, and tools can be tucked away in the eaves closets. This move was quite a jolt for the two teenage boys. Although Father had a job in the factory awaiting him and Mother would be too busy about the house to miss her friends, the boys must start out Monday morning into a strange and alien world— unfriendly streets, a new school, new faces, strange teachers.

That first day of school, when the two boys near the center of town, they are attracted by a large modernistic house. They pause a moment to admire the beautiful beds of roses. The garage doors open and out into the splendor of the morning sun glide twelve cylinders of shimmering chrome and blue. The man at the wheel gives them a friendly nod as he turns into the street. "Wow, what a car!" "What a house!" "Who do you suppose lives there?" Such were their comments. Thoughts of their own futures played across their minds, erasing for an instant the strangeness of their situation. Within a week the boys had a sense of belonging. They made friends among whom was the son of the man who drove the handsome automobile and lived in the great house. The whole town knew about Billy's dad. He had studied law in the East. Now he was president of the Savings and Loan Company, had plenty of money and a speedboat on the river. Some said he might be the next mayor of the town. Oh, he was very successful!

First impressions are often lasting ones. For Harry and Sam the weeks, the months, the years were full of activity. But always there was the thought that some day—some day they, too, would have a home and a car with plenty of chrome, and a speedboat on the river. They wanted to be successful also.

How long ago that first day seemed. Today the Rowe brothers are graduating from high school: Sam with highest honors; Harry just made it. The great question is, should both boys go to college? Sam, certainly. But what about Harry? Poor Harry.

Freshman year was over. Sam as usual was leading his class. The long hours of painful study had been too much for Harry. He wouldn't be returning in the fall. Now there was only one dream—of a great house, and a large car, and a speedboat on the river. Poor Harry.

Twenty years have passed. There is a new name on the door of the Vice-President's office at the Savings and Loan Company. The name is Samuel Rowe. There is a new house in the new sub-division, a new boat on the river, a new name is being suggested for mayor of Circleville—the name of Samuel Rowe, successful businessman, prominent citizen.

But there are other thoughts in the library at Rowe mansion. The new tycoon is thinking, "This town is getting me. Too tame. No cultural advantages. Why didn't I accept that offer to teach? Wouldn't it have been better to have practiced law in the city? Now I'm stuck. Debts, obligations—everyone bothering me about something." He can't sleep. Needs a vacation—can't afford it; too many bills. "Successful citizen!"

Harry is a failure according to the accepted standards—a nobody. But at least he is happy. "Always did want to tinker with cars, that boy. Good mechanic, Harry, but so drab!"

Something is radically wrong with this picture. Why should two men embrace the same dream and both of them be broken by it? Why should two lives try to conform to the same pattern and neither of them fit? I think we know what is wrong. We have been placing so much emphasis on the pattern we have forgotten the capacities of the persons. This pattern of Success is the standard one, with only incidental variations. It has been a stumbling block to many a life incapable of achieving it. The same pattern has become a millstone, stunting the growth, dwarfing the potentialities of many a person who might have risen far above it in service and happiness. Yet there it remains. The conventional pattern of Success—a large home—money—position—prestige —influence.

Once a boy in His father's carpenter shop discovered the futility of trying to drive square pegs into round holes. Later he applied that lesson to human lives. This is what He said about it: "Be not conformed to the things of this world but be ye transformed by the renewing of your minds."

Success is not a series of things to be acquired. It is a life to be lived. Your life or mine. They were never meant to be lived according to man-made standards of success or failure. They have a divine origin. Only the Eternal Plan is adequate to shape them.

We often hear it said that our country suffers from lack of leadership. I don't think so. The leadership is there. It is simply bogged down in the hopeless mediocrity of a pint-sized standard of values.

Sometimes we are betrayed at other points by our desire to conform to human standards. Today an established maximum of work and a minimum wage have become standardized. And well they should be. Out of our American-Christian heritage there has arisen an appreciation of human life that exceeds the value given to it by any other nation or people in the world. We do well to safeguard human life against exhaustion and overwork. But now a new danger threatens us—the danger of meaninglessness that comes of conformity to man-made standards. Work that is completely reduced to the mere consideration of hours and wages has lost its ability to be creative and its incentive to serve.

Achievement in science has come from the souls and minds of those whose first concern was to reach out beyond the conformity of knowledge into the unknown. We owe a great debt for example to those men and women whose greatest desire was not wages and hours but to spend themselves in medical research that they might bring to all of us the means of eliminating pain and restoring health. This constant flow of blessing is ours because there are lives wherein success and achievement are evaluated on the higher level of service and creativeness.

Our age today suffers from stunted standards of goodness which are also man-made. American humanitarianism has borrowed a great many of the spiritual fruits from the tree of Christian faith, much to our benefit. The standard of good American citizenship includes: kindness, honesty, charitable giving; the care of children, the sick, and aged; the rescue of the fallen. We have formulated them into a standard of goodness which is noble and almost unique in a world suddenly grown barbaric. These principles are a part of our community life, subject only to our will to put them into practice for others. If a person conforms to these standards he is considered good. If he fails, he is regarded with some question, and justifiably so. Occasionally we discover an individual who is a failure at the point of practical goodness but who still maintains an active relationship with the Christian Church. He seems to have forgotten that the great Founder translated these ethical principles into human action. Observing this mutation in this modern superficial Christian, the casual observer may say, "I'm just as good a Christian as that fellow and I don't go to church at all." Granted! Our critical friend, however, has missed the point completely. His success as an ethical behaviorist has gone to his head. The real issue is this. How much the more might our "good man" do were he to add to his goodness the strength of will and of heart that comes of living the plan of God, instead of meeting the passing standard of a passing age of world citizens? What great heights of growth in spirit and in love and in brotherhood might we achieve, were all who are sensitive to goodness to make it the transforming characteristic of life instead of the conforming one. It will take more than a man's will to do this. It will take the man plus the Grace of God.

There is an old story of three men who were given certain responsibilities by their governor—each according to his capacity to make use of them. "To one he gave five talents, to another two, and to another one." The man of least responsibility made light of his trust, and buried his talent in the ground because he was offended at the small credit which was given his capabilities. When the day of accounting came, those who had received the larger sums of money gave proof of their trust. They returned twice the amount that was expected of them and were consequently given opportunities for further service. The third man had simply conformed to the standard of the day. He returned his talent just as it was. This man lost his opportunity for service.

To conform to human standards, whether they be of material success, or of work, or of goodness, is to risk contentment with low objectives on the one hand, and failure on the other. Neither is worthy of the possibilities which lie in a man.

We must return now to the really successful man in our story—Harry Rowe, the mechanic. This boy's failure in college did not prove his undoing. Perhaps wise parents remembered the mechanical toys, the tools in the storage space of the bedroom. Perhaps they helped him to see that "the secret of success in life is known to those who have not succeeded." Somehow this lad raised his eyes to higher goals than the ones which captivated him in childhood.

Harry Rowe sings at his work today. His skilled hands can take the old and make it as new. They can take the new untempered metal and fashion it into motors that will serve for many hours. He has carried his skill into his home and applied it to his life. Just the other day he helped his crying son over a hazard on the road to success. With his skilled hands he demonstrated to the lad an easier way to fix the broken toy. Then he said, "Son, don't ever let the thing you can't do keep you from doing what you can do."

The following Sunday Harry had an answer for the question a man in his Bible class had asked. "What does Christ mean by 'Be ye perfect'?" the man queried. Harry had to dig for the answer. In one of his books on the Bible he discovered the Greek word for "perfect" means "the end." He thought about it, and about his own life, which began with a failure. Some might still regard it so, even poor Sam. But he had happiness at the end. "Perfect"—"the end"—that's it. It's not the beginning, but the end that determines success.

An unknown writer gives us the same clue to happiness. He bids us be not "conformed" but "transformed":

THE VICTOR

I saw them start, an eager throng
All young, and strong, and fleet

Joy lighted up their beaming eyes,
Hope sped their flying feet
And one among them so excelled
In courage, strength and grace
That all men smiled and gazed and cried
The winner of the race.

The way was long, the way was hard;
The golden goal gleamed far
Above the distant hills. A shining pilot star.
On they sped, but while some fell,
Some faltered in their speed;
He upon whom all eyes were fixed
Still proudly kept the lead.

But ah, What folly! see, he stops
To raise a fallen child,
To place it out of danger's way
With kiss and warning mild.
A fainting comrade claims his care.
Once more he turns aside;
Then stays his strong young steps to be
A feeble woman's guide.

And so wherever duty calls, or sorrow or distress
He leaves his chosen path to aid,
To comfort and to bless.
Tho man may pity, blame or scorn,
No envious pang may swell—
The soul who yields for love, the place he
Might have won so well.

The race is o'er. Mid shouts and cheers
I saw the victors crowned;
Some wore fame's laurels, some love's flowers
Some brows with gold were bound,
But all unknown, unheeded stood—

Heaven's light upon his face,
With empty hands and uncrowned head,
The winner of the race.

O God, give me strength to live another day. Let me not turn coward before its difficulties or prove recreant to its duties. Let me not lose faith in my fellow men. Keep me sweet and sound of heart, in spite of ingratitude, treachery, or meanness. Preserve me from minding little strings or giving them. Help me to keep my heart clean, and to live so honestly and fearlessly that no outward failure can dishearten me or take away the joy of conscious integrity. Open wide the eyes of my soul that I may see good in all things. Grant me this day some new vision of thy truth, inspire me with the spirit of joy and gladness, and make me the cut of strength to suffering souls; in the name of the strong Deliverer, our only Lord and Saviour, Jesus Christ.

Work and the Kingdom
of God

I WANT YOU to meet a man who has been leading two lives. He wasn't aware of this fact until about a month ago when a friend called it to his attention. Sam Brown was an unhappy man, all mixed-up, ready to quit his job. Tonight he has found himself—and happiness.

It was Friday morning. As usual, Sam was up at six, ready for another day of work. One of the bright spots in the morning was breakfast with his family. As he lingered over his second cup of coffee, the children monopolized the conversation with small talk about school and the coming weekend. Here was enthusiasm and warmth, friendly banter; how keen was their mother's understanding of childhood's little tragedies and joys. Now he must leave this fellowship for a long and unrelished day.

Traffic is heavy this morning. Everyone seems to be hurrying to keep appointments with job and time clock. There are ugly looks at the traffic light. Reckless drivers monopolizing the road. Already the parking lot at the plant is filling up. Sam made it with seconds to spare; and a scratched fender to show for his trouble. In a matter of minutes he moved from a warm and friendly world into a

cold and competitive world. The monotonous jangle of the
time clock! Grumbling workmen in the locker room! The
clamor of the assembly line! Piece upon piece; work against
time. "Careful there, let's do it right while we're at it." Every
fender that passes his station means more profit for the company. Wonder if the union was able to get that raise. Sam
is still paying bills that accumulated during the strike.
"Ouch, my wrist!" "Take it easy. There's a new man at the
next station." "Wonder if he's a stool pigeon."

Rest period brings the usual chorus of gripes. New plant
regulations, more overtime. Better be sure we get time-and-
a-half. Back again at the same old grind. How the hours
drag! Fenders, fenders. Many men, yet he's alone in his
thoughts. Better pay, less work. I'll look out for myself. Just
don't let those hillbillies take all our jobs.

Quitting time can't come too soon. The lonely man,
tired from the tensions of the day, turns his back on job and
time clock. Man against man. Union against management.
Man against danger. Man against traffic. He hates the job.
Grim and full of unpleasant thoughts about trying another
plant, he sits silently down to dinner.

Today is Saturday. Sam awakens in his other, happier,
family world. This is a day of rest. He and his son arose
early. Together they're digging out a new room in the basement of the house. For weeks they've been at it . . . heavy
work . . . long hours . . . but Sam doesn't mind. He's thinking of the warm little house with a new furnace. There'll be
space for his tools; there'll be the cooling spray of a new
shower for the warm summer evenings. How time flies. No
worry about hours and wages here. There are other things
of more value. Sam looks ahead and dreams of the completed job and of what it will mean to the family. He'll take
pride in showing it to the neighbors. He'll tell them, "We
did it ourselves." What if he is tired? A fellow doesn't mind
if he's happy.

Tonight a happy family enjoys its evening meal and makes plans for Sunday: church in the morning, and then an afternoon with friends in the country.

Can this be the same man we saw yesterday? Quite the same! But something has happened to him. A different energy is at work in the home which transforms all of his labor, all of his interests. It is the energy of love.

On the way to church Sam is thinking, "I wish that the automotive plant were like my family. If we could all pull together, if we all cared about one another, if we could just see the whole plan and feel a part of it. Two worlds—they just don't fit together."

What a strange coincidence that the Bible lesson should be about a man who went out to hire laborers for his vineyard, from the 20th Chapter of St. Matthew. The story tells how at the end of the day there was the usual disagreement about wages and hours. Men who worked all day got their wages according to contract, but those who worked half a day received the same. Some worked only an hour. They, too, received a day's wages.

In the pew behind Sam sits the plant manager. He, too, needs this story.

The rector observes that this was not a story about labor and management. It is a lesson about people and their needs. It is an example of a man who cared not only about his workmen, but about all people. He was concerned about fair wages for workers; but also that each of them should have enough on which to live. Furthermore, this man assumed a responsibility for the unemployed.

This, the rector said, was an example of the kind of relationships that our Lord proposed in what He called the Kingdom of God, or "the Kingdom of right relationships." Then Christianity *is* interested in work and human needs. But even more, it is concerned about human happiness. This employer treated his workmen as a father would deal with his children—on the basis of affection and love. He was looking ahead. If only a few worked, the others would have to beg or rob or steal if they became desperate. Sam hoped the workmen in the story saw this, too. Perhaps when they came back the next day, all were ready to do the work together, each bearing a part of the responsibility of the needy and the unemployed. Jesus had pictured industry, all life, to be like a family in which the energy of concern for one another is stronger than the demands of any group or any one person.

Of course, this fits into His rule for living. "That ye love one another as I have loved you."

Sam Brown made his own application. The family shares its love, its responsibility, its work, its earnings. The family has its householder, the mother, who works for a higher purpose than income alone. She sees the future, and what it must yield for all the members of the family. Her life is richer than hours or wages. Hers is a stewardship, a trust. Gradually the children are uplifted by her spirit to share their lives with one another in a little "Kingdom of right relationships."

Sam also learns that there is another family—here together, this Sunday morning. Their offerings are placed on the same alms basin—Sam Brown's, the plant manager's, and those of others as well—gifts to express their common belief in a common Lord. They are the Church. This family works together, prays together for the great family of all men. Sam and his employer now serve on the same vestry. They're committeemen for the scout troop to which their sons belong. Each has learned a new respect and appreciation for the other. Before they leave church, they sing the same hymn:

> Forth in Thy Name, O Lord, I go my daily labor to
> pursue—
> Thee, only Thee, resolved to know, in all I think
> or speak or do.

When Sam leaves church, a single thought goes with him: Is it possible to develop this feeling of family at the automotive plant?

Monday morning has a new interest for Sam. He is thinking about the Kingdom of Right Relationships. The driver of the car at the intersection is a member of a family, working for the same goals as he. In the locker room he finds another member of his Church who'd worked for years at this same plant. Even his job is less forbidding today. That fender might be placed on the new automobile that would take a workman and his family on a well-earned vacation, or it might carry blood plasma to one in surgery, or milk to his home, or food to a stricken village. That new man in the next section—could he be one who is working for the first time in many weeks? If so, how good it must seem to be "off relief."

At the union meeting Sam accepted an assignment on the bargaining committee. There'd be no strike if he could help it. Surely wage agreements could be worked out by men who belong to the same Christian family. He discovered he didn't dislike the boss any more, nor was he a man to be feared. What seemed to concern him most was the determination to do everything in his power to make the Kingdom of Right Relationships come alive right here in the automotive plant. Some of the boys may think he's queer, but he'll take a chance on that. Sam wasn't tired Monday night. Talk to him today and he'll tell you, "I like my work. You see, I'm living just one life now."

What happened to Sam Brown can happen—must happen—all over this great nation.

Never in our history has the need of a family relationship in industry weighed so heavily upon us. We need a long, broad view of ourselves as one people and of our need to work cooperatively.

Work in the factory means a margin of profit to replace equipment that will keep a maximum number of men employed. Workingmen buy food, clothing, automobiles which keep other thousands of men on an income basis. Work stoppage in Buffalo, Cleveland, Pittsburgh, or Minneapolis, can start a chain reaction that might ruin us economically, spreading chaos and disaster. Men of differing nationalities and religious backgrounds are a part of this great family, with needs to be met and contributions to make, provided job opportunities are given to them. Many of them have come to us at the eleventh hour, needing nothing so much as a chance. Along our streets, day after day, trudge elderly people with excellent skills but without work. All these are our responsibility. They are the problem of both labor and management. Unemployed persons mean greater relief loads and bread lines. Such emergency measures mean higher taxes for those who do work.

A man and his job have new dignity and a new worth today. They become meaningful in the highest sense as we see them related to other work and other lives. They are the inner fortress of the nation.

One day three men engaged in the same construction project were asked this question: "What are you doing?"

The first replied, "I'm mixing cement."

The second answered, "I'm earning $2.00 an hour."

The third workman, looking up at the structure before him said, "I'm building a Cathedral."

If one is to have such a view as this of his work, one must have also the quality of love-energy that is in the family and in the Christian Church. To build a family in industry calls for a common purpose and a common concern.

Leslie Weatherhead said this about the Kingdom of Right Relationships: "Within the family of God things work out like this. They do not work out thus in a pagan industry."

A century ago in northern Europe stood an old cathedral upon one of the arches of which was carved a face of great beauty. It has a remarkable story. When the cathedral was being built, it is said, an elderly man came seeking work. Because of his age and probably unsteady hand, the foreman gave him a little job high on the arch, where no eye might see the imperfection of his work. Here he labored singing at his work, until one day the noise of his hammer stopped. They found him asleep in death, his face upturned toward his carving, an exquisite likeness of someone he had known and loved. When the workmen assembled they beheld no inferior work, but a masterpiece. They said, "This is the grandest work of all; for love wrought this."

It was love that gave singleness and joy to the healing, unifying work of Sam Brown, automotive worker—the love of God. This same love, spread abroad from heart to heart, will transfigure all our working hours and relationships. Force will not do it. Hate cannot do it. But,

> When on the sweat of labour and its sorrow,
>   Toiling in twilight, flickering and dim,
> Flames out the sunshine of the great tomorrow,
>   When all the world looks up—because of Him.
>
> Then will He come—with meekness for His glory
>   God in a workman's jacket as before,
> Living again the Eternal Gospel Story,
>   Sweeping the shavings from His workshop floor.
>   —*G. A. Studdert Kennedy*

Teach us good Lord to serve thee as thou deservest; to give and not to count the cost; to fight and not to heed the wounds; to toil and not to seek for rest; to labor and not to ask for any reward save that of knowing we do thy will.

The House that Hate Built

PROPAGANDA

THIS IS the story of the house that hate built. It is not the conventional type of house, set on a street, with doors, windows, and a shingled roof. It is located high on a rock ledge, carved out of a cliff. Its small openings are scarcely large enough for a man to enter. Only a dim light penetrates the tiny window slots. The front porch is a ladder of vines reaching down to the valley and used only by the people who live in the cave and who draw it up behind them when they enter their home.

The family that lives in this house is unlike any we have ever known. Clad in the skin of a beast and barefoot, their stout bodies are browned by sun and weather. The grownups move noiselessly in the twilight of the cave, exchanging only an occasional guttural word or a suspicious glance. The children, like frightened little animals, crouch in the shadowy corners, reflecting the fear that is written so deeply on the faces of their elders. Life for each of them is a matter of survival. Any stranger is to them a potential enemy looking for shelter and food—their food. So it is kill or be killed. That wall of stone and this heavy club are the only defense against the cruel march of the jungle. Many centuries ago this was a home—one of the best. It was designed by fear and ignorance; it was built by hate.

Today the cave is gone, and with it, the frightened skin-clad barbarian. In the valleys and across the plain stand homes by the thousands, blazing with light, doors with latches on the outside. There are children who laugh and play together, neighbors who respect and trust one another. People are free to speak as they wish, to live where they choose, to unite in cooperative enterprise for the good of all. Man has almost forgotten his basic "urge to survive." Life is taken for granted. Today's struggle is to live abundantly, without fear. Instead of a club, laws govern our relationships. Knowledge and research have hurled back the frontier of ignorance. A man, looking about him at the peaceful countryside, will say, "It's great to be alive! See what we have been able to do!"

There is good reason for pride in today's achievements. But let's not put on those rose-colored glasses just yet. Hidden away in the attics of these fine homes, covered with the dust of time, rests the animal skin, and beside it, the caveman's club. Down in the deepest recesses of the mind the law of the jungle survives. Time and circumstances have changed. The man has merely adjusted himself to them. Strip him of knowledge, rob him of his abundance, deny him the resources of spiritual power, and soon—alarmingly soon —there appears the barbarian, looking for a cave in which to hide.

Out of this age of brilliance and progress and civilization, please note these accomplishments: Gas chambers for the extermination of peoples; mass murder; death by starvation; slave labor; the erasing of cities; total war and in its wake, hollow-eyed, fear-driven, ragged survivors who must forage for food and struggle against one another to survive. This is a familiar design. Do you remember? Its architects are fear and ignorance. Because of them, men must live in "the house that hate built."

This fact of our nature modern civilized man has ignored or forgotten at times. Yet there have been many evidences that fear and ignorance continue to produce hate. "He" may wear a suit of conservative gray, and "She" may wear the latest Paris gown. They are a charming couple to their friends. Others, beyond their exclusive circle, know from experience that the cave and the club are still there.

"He" dislikes certain people because of their nationality. "She" is very much afraid of those people with "green hair." Why? He has heard rumors that those people whose ancestors came from that nation control all the money. If they take his savings he will have no security. So he nods his head in agreement with those who say, "It's the fault of those people that the country is in such a mess. They ought to be sent back where they came from." It never occurs to our friend that the people he fears, and later hates, have made greater contributions to American life—have a better record of patriotism, and a finer record of humanitarianism—than people of his own ancestry. But he needs a scapegoat.

"She" is afraid of the people with "green hair" because they are different in appearance. Her friends have known some of these green-haired people who were lazy or dirty or dishonest or uncultured. So she brands all green-haired people as guilty of the same defects. Of course, she doesn't know any of them personally, but one "can't be too careful these days." Her hatred is the result of ignorance. So she uses what we call the stereotype as a cave in which to hide.

Here are civilized people, victims of the Stone Age emotions: fear and hate. As a result, everybody suffers. There is no peace; no one is safe from discrimination who lives in the house that hate built. When men hate each other, then anything can happen and anything goes.

The fact that our Stone Age emotions are so easily

aroused represents a great opportunity for those interested in world conquest. A Mongolian warlord named Ghengis Khan used a simple technique with devastating effectiveness to weaken and subdue his enemies. This was his scheme: "Pit race against race, religion against religion, class against class—divide and conquer."

During World War II America was flooded with stories, rumors, literature, and lies designed to achieve this end. For, we remember, we were on the time schedule of a would-be world conqueror.

Here is a typical example. Shortly after Pearl Harbor this story was told as humorous. "The first man to have sunk an enemy battleship was a flier named Fitzharris. The first man to have received a purple heart medal was a man named O'Grady. The first man to have won an oak leaf cluster was a man named McGonnigal. But the first man to have cashed a war bond was a man named Levine." I hope you didn't laugh at this story or retell it. For it originated in the propaganda machine of Hitler's "German Reich." It was designed to turn Jew against Roman Catholic, and to discredit Jews in general, so that a double portion of hate would make a rift in the relationship between these two splendid segments of our society and thus weaken American solidarity. Other similar stories were circulated to produce fear and hate. Europeans were hoodwinked into hating Asiatics. Labor was pitted against management, Negroes against whites, by enemy propaganda. "Divide and conquer."

Today we are being subjected to an even greater and more effective campaign to produce hate and strife among us. Almost every medium of communication is being used: rumor, gossip, the spoken word, the telephone, television, radio, the official documents of government agencies. Comic books, petitions, printed literature, anonymous letters, movies—each may carry its venomous message to build in our minds a house of hate.

May we suggest a few simple methods for the detection of such dangerous material?

1. Does the information you have received incite you to fear or anger against a group? This is another example of the stereotype.

2. Does the material you have read present a particular type of person in an unfavorable light, making you suspicious of the intentions of all such people? Are they portrayed consistently as gangsters, thugs, criminals, disloyal citizens? If so, you may be observing an attempt to make scapegoats out of a people, who, as a group, are no more blameworthy than other groups.

3. Does the information before you attempt to discredit and ridicule the American system of government? Who published it?

4. Is the story you have just heard true? or is it only hearsay? Where did the teller hear it? Ask for the facts, or get them from your Board of Community Relations.

5. A word of caution is now necessary. Because any one or all of the means of communication might be used by propagators of hate, this does not mean we are to regard any one medium with suspicion. Ours is still the land of free speech and free press. They who would crush freedom and distort knowledge are at liberty to use our most legitimate means of communication to carry their message. It is our responsibility and privilege to sift and evaluate the propaganda.

6. We should like to suggest one further standard by which to test your information. In the material before you, what is the value of a man? Does the writer promise you lavish rewards, power, and influence? Does he use your situation of need or neglect to offer you a rosy future, free of all worry, with guaranteed security at little or no cost to yourself? The road to tyranny and slavery has been paved with

the "fools' gold" of impossible promises offered to desperate people. Look beyond the promise. What is the situation of the people of the world who have accepted that offer? Look at Hungary, at Poland, at China, at Tibet.

America is far from a paradise for many people. But it is still the land of greatest hope. Here power doesn't go unchecked. Here human rights are defended by law. Here goodness is commended and evil is ultimately exposed and punished. If there are failures, the defects are not of the system, but of its misuse by individuals.

The religious heritage which fostered the American way of life sees man as of value as an individual. He was created by God, and therefore he has the right to be protected and aided by his fellow man.

Religion also says that hate, ignorance and fear can turn this man into a self-centered tyrant or a cave man with a club. Therefore, he needs the discipline and love of his fellow man and of God to enable him to find and achieve his rightful place in life. This is the opportunity America offers you and me—a chance to be free of the darkness of the house that hate built. In the spirit of our founding fathers, and by the road of honest effort, of faith and responsibility, we may find the way through Him who said: "Ye shall know the truth, and the truth shall make you free."

Come out of that cave!

Almighty God, who hast made us all of one blood, give to us, we beseech thee, the will to labor for good will and co-operation among the people of the world. Put away from us all pride and prejudice, all selfish ambition; help us to pursue only those ends and purposes that will promote unity and concord and further the coming of thy kingdom in the earth; through Jesus Christ, our Lord.

Happiness

IF THERE had to be a quarrel in the Squabble family, it's a good thing for the neighborhood that it occurred in the winter. Closed doors and windows have muffled the unpleasant sound of angry voices. The world doesn't need to know it, but Fred and Amy Squabble are in trouble. It all seemed to start the other night. Fred came home late from work— at least that's what he told Amy. He knew it was the day her bridge club met. Dinner would be late—leftovers again, probably. Amy would be tired and irritable and full of the afternoon's gossip. A lot of small talk about how important the Smiths are, and about the winter vacation the Jones are taking. No use listening to that chatter; he might as well stop off for a hand or two of poker at Ollie's. It was a dull game. No luck. Too bad he had to lose that twenty. How did it get to be quarter of eight? Yes, he could drive all right. The remainder of that evening hadn't been pleasant either for Fred or Amy. A few curt exchanges of conversation during dinner, an alibi, a complaint, a grumbled response, some tears, an hour or two repairing fishing tackle, a restless night, then next morning a glum breakfast of coffee and aspirin.

Tonight started peacefuly enough until plans for New Year's eve became the topic of discussion. Amy remembered last year. She suggested they do something different—such a waste of money to sit and eat and watch poor entertainment. Besides none of her friends were there, and who wants to talk fishing all the time?

It was at this point that Fred lost control of himself. That evening had cost him plenty last year. This is what he gets. No appreciation. No understanding—just nag, nag, and tears. What's the use!

The neighbors didn't hear this quarrel, nor did they see Fred drive away. But they had known for a long time that a storm was brewing. They remembered those first years when Fred and Amy were newlyweds. They wonder what has become of the courteous and attractive youth who responded so easily to his charming wife. Can this surly, demanding, self-centered individual be the same person? What has happened to the attractive young lady who once enjoyed a hike or an outing with her husband? Can this haggling, whining, negativistic woman be the same person? Here, ten years away from their marriage a selfish, surly man and an equally selfish woman have grown apart. They disagree about their friends. They dislike each other's hobbies; their attitude toward life in general is in conflict. For the past several years they have known something was wrong. They have tried to escape their differences by an occasional lavish spree. Or the man has tried to bribe his way back into his wife's good graces by means of occasional gifts. Or they have faced each New Year with a sense of regret and a half-hearted resolution to turn over a new leaf. But a week or more has found them deep in the old rut—self-centered, quarrelsome, unhappy.

What can be done about it? Must these two maladjusted souls follow their separate paths down the desolate road to loneliness and a broken home? Must their children pay the price of their parents' failure? Shall they be condemned to carry the scar of the wound that was inflicted on them by lives without love? There is much that can be done for people like Fred and Amy. In fact, there is much that they can do.

1. First, they have to want to solve their problem. How often it is that families in this kind of difficulty refuse to do anything about it until it is too late and they no longer care. If they do really want to correct their situation, there must be a willingness on the part of each of them to face the fact that there *is* a problem and that both man and wife are part of it. Just as it takes two people to make a marriage, so it takes two people to wreck one.

2. It is of the utmost importance at this point that each shall see himself as he really is. This is difficult for a person with a grievance to do. Many persons have found great value in a third point of view about their problem. Any modern city is rich in resources to assist our troubled families. Some have found their clergyman helpful in providing a neutral, yet sympathetic, outlook on their difficulty. Others have used the services of a family counselling agency where trained personnel are prepared to offer clinical help. Your Council of Social Agencies or your pastor can easily refer you to such an agency.

3. Fred and Amy need to recognize that it is they who must face their problem and come to grips with it. There are those who are qualified to analyze the difficulty; but a third person can't heal the rift, nor will it heal itself. One dares not ignore it. Nor can he run away from it. I should like to suggest a plan of self-examination and a course of action— something husband and wife can do together in the interest of preventing marital catastrophe:

(a) Discover and keep constantly before you the factors which produce happiness in any home. Some years ago two instructors at Columbia University made a survey to determine what makes happiness in a marriage. They carefully questioned a large number of married couples in order to present if possible, the major reasons for happiness or lack of it. They found that three questions gave them the most helpful information: (1) Do you agree in your philosophy of life? That is, do you both place the same value on each other, on children, on money, on God, on pleasure? (2) Do you agree on your friends? (3) Do you enjoy the same pastimes and recreations? Where the answer to each question was Yes, the researchers found greater happiness prevailed. Where the answer to each was No, they found great unhappiness. How do *you* answer these three questions? And what are you willing to do about bringing them into agreement?

(b) What is your objective as an individual. Is it *to make* someone happy? Or is it *to be made* happy by someone? There is an old formula which says that marriage is a 50-50 proposition. I think we should change that saying, for it is basically false. We need to state it this way: Happy marriage requires all there is of two persons. There can be no dividing line. Each must be willing to go all of the way all the time.

(c) The third question in the check-yourself test is this. Have you made allowances for the fact that you are, and always will be, two distinct and separate personalities? Marriage was never intended to force two people into a single personality mould. Its design is "they two shall become one flesh"—one family; that the two persons shall use such understanding and self-discipline as is necessary to blend their lives into unity of purpose and effort. Of primary importance, then, is it that we discover just what kind of personalities we have to interweave and that we then make the adjustments necessary to do that.

(d) In any average family there will be disagreements. The question is: Have you learned to deal with these differences as they arise? In other words, have you learned to "quarrel constructively"? We do need an opportunity to air our views.

We need someone to whom and with whom we can give expression to our feelings. What better person can each choose than one's husband or wife? Everyday life affords few opportunities for this kind of mental release. The home can become a safety valve when man and wife are free to "talk it out" without the danger of hurt feelings. Such occasions can be of tremendous value to both. Suppose there *are* differences of opinion. Is it not better to express them and understand each other's views than to suppress them and build permanent barriers? Choose a moment of calm when you can discuss not the difference, but the cause of the difference quietly and free of emotion and then agree on the constructive steps which can be taken to eliminate the cause.

(e) Do you love your partner enough to confess your shortcomings (which she already knows) and seek each other's help and forgiveness in overcoming them? A small boy was once required to give the definition of "friend." He replied, "Oh, he's a fellow who knows all about you and likes you just the same." May it not well be said of husband or wife—that each knows all about the other, yet loves the other just the same?

(f) Have you added the plus of Religion to your family life? The Columbia University tests for happiness revealed one more important fact. Where there was an active faith in God expressed by both husband and wife in regular worship, their agreement on friends, pastimes, and values reached its supreme height. As a consequence, the tests proved the old adage to be overwhelmingly true: "Church-attending families are happier families."

Suppose Fred and Amy were to make such a study of themselves tomorrow and find, as they undoubtedly would, that each must make certain definite and drastic changes in his personal conduct, habits, attitudes, and outlook on life.

What is their next step? Shall they follow the pattern of past frustrations by making a New Year's resolution which they cannot keep? At the beginning of each year we wish that we might begin our actions on the note of our high resolve, and continue it throughout the year ahead. But somehow the end of a twelve-month period finds us far from the line of our original purpose. So we begin again, and each year regret that we have been forced to make such a wide detour. The familiar axiom says, "A straight line is the shortest distance between two points." Instead of a straight line of progress, our lives seem to run a zig zag course.

Let's face the fact. The past is inescapable. This year's chapter will be based upon the last. This year's conduct, principles, and thoughts, while tempered by a new day, new friends, and new situations, is inseparably tied to yesterday. Whether that past shall be a blessing or a curse depends upon whether it has produced good or evil, happiness or unhappiness. Occasionally we find a man or woman whose will is strong enough to break with the past and follow the straight line. But the majority of us are like Fred and Amy. If our lives are in a rut, we either resign ourselves to it and burrow deeper, or we make feeble and fruitless excuses—"I am what I am," or "you just can't change human nature."

The believing man has come nearer the answer to the problem of new beginnings. He says, "You can't change human nature, but God *can*." There has opened to him a means of making that new beginning permanent. He has found that he spends in real self-examination half the time he used to spend worrying or making excuses for himself, and he also realizes that his problem needs spiritual help. The problems of the home are resolvable if love and forgiveness are there to help us face and overcome them. The shortcomings of a person require God's Grace and Forgiveness. St. Paul once analyzed his personal problem in these words. "The good that I would I do not. The evil that I would not that I do. Wretched man that I am, who shall deliver me from the body of this death?" His faults hung upon him like a deadly weight. But because he recognized his need to be a spiritual one, he sought and found spiritual help. His discovery of the Source of help turned his despair into a cry of victory. "I thank God, through Jesus Christ." Here if ever is the Unfailing Friend, who "knows all about us and loves us just the same."

Christ is saying to us, "Come up out of that low-vaulted past into the magnificent expanse of a New Year's possibilities, opportunities, and hopes. The walk with Me is in newness of life; My service is in newness of spirit." He bids us, as He did His other disciples, let the dead past be its own undertaker, and take with us on our way only the past's legitimate legacy—its experience and its lessons. To this we must add the reassurance Christ gives to anyone who will accept His help: "My Grace is sufficient for you."

Whether the happiness we seek tomorrow is for our own family or for an individual struggling under a burden of habit, or whether that happiness is for a newly freed man, striving to make a comeback within the law, or for a child reaching up from the confusion of adolescence toward manhood—whether the call to happiness is to you or to me, the formula is the same. Take a good look at yourself. Accept what you find. Then commit it to God. Reach out and take the opportunity that God all along has been offering you. Walk forward with Him into His new day.

Since it is of thy mercy, O gracious Father, that another day is added to our lives, we here dedicate both our souls and our bodies to Thee and Thy service, in a sober, righteous and godly life; in which resolution, do Thou, O merciful God, confirm and strengthen us; that as we grow in age, we may grow in grace, and in the knowledge of our Lord and Saviour Jesus Christ.

Brotherhood — American Style

In an earlier chapter we spoke about the house that hate built. Now I want to tell you about some friends of mine who live in a house that love built. Let's visit with them a few minutes. The slender young lady who answers the door is Elaine. "Yes, the whole family are at home. Won't you come in?" Behind her stands a young boy who is curious about the arriving guests. We are somewhat amazed to learn that this stocky blackeyed lad is Alphonse. But we are due for more surprises. In the living room we meet Frederick. He is a tall young man of athletic build, his features unlike those of either his sister or brother. We look in vain for some resemblance to one of the parents. There is none whatsoever. Here are five individuals each strikingly different from the other. Yet we know from our brief visit that they belong in this house. They are one family. They attend the same church. They share a common life and a common affection. There is family interest in Elaine's coming birthday. All are concerned about Fred's 70 in English.

At this point the children excuse themselves. They are off together to attend a basketball game.

Father and mother fill the inquisitive silence with a burst of conversation. They have sensed our bewilderment.

They pour out an unusual story of mingled pathos and happiness. This is what they have to say:

"These children are not ours by birth. They were sent to us during the war years. Ours was a rather lonely house, with no children. A friend told us about Elaine. It was in 1941 that we sent for her. She is Norwegian. Her parents were killed during the German occupation. What a joy it has been to watch her once thin little face grow chubby with proper nourishment and to see the look of fear leave those great blue eyes. It was two years later we learned about Alphonse and Fred. We saw their pictures in a folder about displaced persons. Within a matter of months they came to join us. Now we have a Norwegian daughter with two brothers, one Spanish and one German—quite an American family, don't you think?"

The real story began at this point. Here were three little rivals for whom life had been a heartbreaking struggle to survive. When they first came to live in this house they snatched one another's food, treated one another with suspicion and open hostility. There were many months of heartache as in each child self-confidence and trust were rebuilt. With what painstaking care each one had to be given his opportunity to share in the privileges and responsibilities of the home.

"Little by little, we saw the rough edges hewn away by patience and experience. With the disappearance of fear and hunger, real personalities began to develop. It was after our first vacation together that we began to feel as if we were really one household. It may have been the lesson we read from the Bible that first Sunday at the lake which marked the turning point. 'Are we not all one family? Hath not one God created us?' Those words seemed to apply to us especially. We learned to play together, to tramp the woods together, to pray together. One night as the two of us were discussing our situation alone, we began to realize how different our lives and interests had become. These children were now a part of us, and we of them. We had given them a home; but they gave us in return a new reason for living. I think you could say we became a real family the day we discovered we loved these children. They became brothers and sisters the day they discovered they were loved with an equal love by the same parents."

We left this home with the feeling that we had witnessed a miracle. As a family what was unusual about it was the circumstances that had created it. Such harmony and happiness can be found in any home where love is in command. This is the house that love built.

We have been thinking all week about another family that needs so desperately this miracle-working ingredient of love. It is the great American family of different races and nationalities. Here, for two centuries we have gathered under one government: refugees and idealists from every part of the world, from England and Spain, from Sweden, Germany, Poland, Italy, Japan, China, and Africa.

To the forefathers of most of us, America was the land of opportunity. Except for those forcibly brought to these shores, so it was. In 1908 Israel Zangwill said, "America is God's crucible, the great melting pot where all the races of Europe are melting and reforming!"

This was true while our population was small and our industries were young. Our ancestors shared their hard-won blessings and thanked God for them. The memory of oppression and want in former surroundings made the rigors of the new land and the new life with its new freedom quite acceptable. Out of hardship there was forged a nation whose leaders determined once and for all to protect the individual man from the danger of tyranny and slavery and hate. This was a happy family with plenty of room for all; with new frontiers to begin a new life whenever a man desired it;

with a strong Constitution and Bill of Rights to guarantee freedom for all.

Then one day the last frontier was crossed. Cities began to spread out toward one another. People crowded into small areas to be near their place for work. Giant factories with mechanical hands could produce more than enough goods to supply the needs of all. Presently wheels stopped turning. Work became scarce. Want and fear made rivals out of any two men seeking one job. The melting pot had grown cold. The family of peoples crowded nearer and nearer the source of shelter and opportunity; but they huddled in groups according to nationality, race, and religion, seeking the protection of their own kind. Suspicion, bad blood, rivalry, clamor for privilege, demand for recognition; the need for decent housing and a fair wage; the rise of crime, discrimination, name calling—all these are symptoms of a desperate people crying out for opportunity.

Do you see what was happening? The "children" were growing up, but not in spirit. Instead of accepting joint responsibilities, they talk only about individual and group rights. They turn deaf ears to people who talk about brotherhood and love. They ignore a Man who gave His life upon a Cross, praying with forgiveness in His heart that "they all may be one." Ignored or forgotten is the tragic lesson of the Civil War, as well as the prophetic words of Lincoln, the statesman and martyr, who said, "We shall either meanly lose or nobly save the last best hope of earth."

Out of the confusing period of the nation's adolescence there suddenly came a unifying power. Within twenty years America was dealt two body blows—World Wars I and II. Rivalries were set aside, and men and women of differing cultures worked, or fought, and died, side by side. Why? Something bigger than any single group had brought these quarreling children together, giving them a sense of joint responsibility, of new affection and loyalty for their adopted fatherland.

Twice, with shouts of joy we welcomed the victors and pledged ourselves to be forever one family, united in the common love of country. But in the years that followed something was lost—the strong incentives of danger and fear. At present there is nothing taking their place. Once more there is rivalry for jobs, name calling, rioting, clamor for laws. And when the legislation is enacted, its enforcement is resisted.

Now suppose your child were beaten and injured . . . not for any wrong she had done, but because of the religious belief of her parents. What would you do? Or suppose you were made the victim of insult and abuse for an act that was ignorantly and falsely blamed on your religious ancestors. What would you do? Or suppose you had laid aside your purple heart decoration and your uniform in exchange for working clothes only to find that your racial heritage was a barrier to an honest income and a decent home. What would you do?

It is not by accident that the eminent historian Toynbee said recently: "No civilization has ever fallen by threats from without." This is not theory, but fact, and as the past three years tragically illustrate, it applies to the American family of people in particular. Our greatest vulnerability is within our boundaries—even in our hearts.

The war years taught us much. We have seen to what heights of unity and loyalty a great emotion will carry us in an emergency. But what will do it in peacetime?

Throughout this land groups of concerned and thinking people have put aside their childish differences to work side by side for harmony and brotherhood. Civil festivals have emphasized the contribution of various cultural groups to our rich heritage and civilization. In some states, laws have been passed to guarantee the basic rights of individuals in employment and housing, regardless of race or creed. Citizens have served as volunteers to mediate explosive situations, and to prepare us to combat the attempts of our enemies to further divide us.

Such efforts have brought us a great distance along the road to harmony and maturity. But the work has been spotty, appealing only to minds ready to receive it. Sometimes we have used "fear of conquest" as a springboard for action against discrimination. Families are not built on fear. They are greatly strengthened, but they cannot be built on education. Families are created, strengthened and sustained by one force only—the force of love.

There is only one love great enough to weld a diversified people into a family or brotherhood. That is a Father's love. European nations tried to achieve this unity with their doctrine of fatherland. Others have appealed to national loyalty which we call patriotism. The very word springs from the Greek "pater" meaning father.

There is only one fatherlove great enough to build a house of love for a nation or for the world. That is the love of God. Hear again the prophet Malachi: "Are we not all one family? hath not one God created us?"

Brotherhood is a family term which only those who live in families where love exists can fully understand.

1. Brotherhood means personal concern and responsibility for the life and well-being of another. Suppose you are informed that a house on Elm Street has burned to the ground. A family has lost all of its possessions. You are moved to impersonal sympathy. But suppose someone tells you it is your brother's house. Immediately you have a personal interest and a sense of responsibility. What a different proposition it is for me to read of an injustice if I regard the victim as my brother.

That family of disciples who were to bring the good news of Christ to every creature in the world received very simple but definite instructions for making their mission succeed. "A new commandment give I unto you—that ye love one another as I have loved you." Those are marching orders that will bring victory wherever men will follow them.

2. The family story sheds light on another responsibility. Brothers have a duty to love even those whose behavior they do not like. There were undoubtedly many things about little Alphonse that Elaine and Fred did not like—attitudes and habits, manners, language. What older boy or girl does not look with some degree of disapproval upon the antics of a child? But a sister or brother claims it as a family responsibility to work for the full development of the youngster. For they want most of all to see him achieve happiness. That's what love is. How did "love" replace "like?" Their parents told us it happened the day the three children discovered they were loved with an equal love by the same father and mother.

So, for the Christian, the knowledge of God's great love of all men makes it possible for brotherhood to rise above difference and dislike.

This has been the foundation of the American plan of life. An individual is sacred because he is a child of God. Therefore we are brothers, intended by God to learn to live by the law of love. Those who have done so have won for themselves the superb prize of happiness.

To this end our laws were formulated. On this principle our government was founded. By this conviction democracy will live. And men will continue to know the blessings of the house built by love. Men who pray together can live together in harmony and peace.

John Oxenham has put this truth into verse:

> In Christ there is no East or West,
> In Him no south or north,

But one great fellowship of love
  Throughout the whole wide earth.

Join hands, then, brothers of the faith,
  Whate'er your race may be!
Who serves my Father as a son
  Is surely kin to me.

This is Brotherhood.

Family Camp

Bill Swann hurried home from work. He let himself in the side door and slipped quietly down the stairs to the basement. The motives for his secrecy were twofold: fishing season was just around the corner, and tackle had to be put into shape; and second, he was not on the best terms with Dolores, his wife. Both of them were touchy these days. Every discussion seemed to lead to an argument. Let's see now, paint, emery stone, graphite, oil . . . Bill was startled by his wife's presence at his elbow. "Dee, look, I'm sorry about last night. Let's quit this infernal quarreling."

Dolores' reply was not what he expected. "Bill, I've an idea. Instead of our usual vacation, let's do something different."

"For instance."

"Well, what would you think of spending week after next at the church family camp?"

Bill was so startled he tipped over a can of paint—"What, a whole week with a church group? Are you cracked? Isn't it enough that you pressure me to go to church every Sunday—well, some Sundays—without handing me this?"

His wife's eyes flashed as she said, "Look! I'm tired of being a fisherman's widow. It's time we started acting like a family—and you began thinking of someone other than your-self for a change."

"Look, Dee," his voice was conciliatory; "You know I've been planning for months to go trout fishing that weekend. Besides when I take some vacation time I really want to do something."

"For instance?"

"Oh, travel, see the country, swim, fish, play golf."

"But we've done that for the last three years. Believe me I know—pack and rush, ride all day, come home tired. I'm sick of it! You know how the children bother you after a week in the car. No thanks, not for me." Neither of them had seen Billie and Anne descend the stairs, so intent were they on their discussion. "Where're we goin'?" Billie inquired.

"Nowhere," replied father, blotting the paint from his work bench. "Mother has a screwy idea we should go to a family camp."

"What's that?" shrilled Anne.

It was Dolores' turn to explain: "Oh, it's a group of families from St. Paul's who want to spend a week together at Camp Carson."

"Who?" queried Anne.

"Oh, Norsons, Becks, Kramers, Staleys and, of course, Mr. Thorpe."

"Never heard of 'em," growled Bill, "except for the preacher."

"Well, I have," explained Junior, "I play with Dickie Norson and Tim Beck every day. Gee, let's go to family camp."

"Yeah, let's," echoed Anne.

"We're not going; and that's final," father declared, and buried himself in his hobby.

But it wasn't final. Two Mondays later a grumbling Bill, his uneasy wife, and two excited children were on their

way to Camp Carson, the family camp owned by St. Paul's
Church. Bill was still protesting, "Ought to have my head
examined—letting you talk me into this crazy scheme."
Dolores, still on the defensive, replied, "I didn't talk you
into it. Remember? Your fishing pals had to work." Then,
in another tone, "Bill, I hope this works out all right." "You
hope! Don't tell me the prospect of mosquitos, ants, poison
ivy, and your 'do-good' friends is giving *you* cold feet."
Neither Bill nor Dolores had more than the vaguest idea of
what might happen at a family camp. Nor did they have
more than superficial knowledge of a church, for that matter.

This was the Swann's second year in Parkside. Like almost everyone else in the neighborhood, they were "time-
payment owners" of a house, a car, a deep freeze, and a color
television. Even the driveway and the landscaping would
"someday be theirs." It was not long before the churches of
the community were after them, offering the whole gamut of
twentieth-century enticements: "the best people," the most
modern classrooms, futuramic architecture, air conditioning,
liberal sermons, and choirs with marimba soloists. After the
Rev. David Thorpe of St. Paul's came to visit, the Swanns,
being nominal Christians, enrolled their children in the
church school. Bill's reasons were pretty blunt, and pretty
superficial: "St. Paul's is only three blocks away. Bill and
Anne can walk it after the first few weeks. You know, padre,
I think a church is a good thing for a community all right.
Children need to learn to be good citizens. But as for me,
I might as well tell you now, I won't be around too much. I
work pretty hard during the week and I need my days off for
recreation. Now don't get me wrong; I'm a good Christian.
Very religious in fact. But I have my own religion. I follow
the ten commandments. Jesus did a pretty good job when He
gave us these." At this point in the conversation David
Thorpe was ready to leave. How many times had he heard
this same sickly patter? As he drove away, one might have

heard him say something like this: "Do-it-yourself religion! They're so much alike, these Parksiders—haven't the slightest idea what it means to be a Christian. Think you can buy character! The nerve of that fellow—ten commandments! Like to see him keep even the first one—"No other gods but Me." No other gods but self and success and status. He didn't even know the ten commandments are a part of the Old Testament. Wonder if he knows there is an Old Testament. Spiritual idiots, these 'my own religion' boys—nothing to hold, nothing to give away. Well, that's why I'm here. But please, dear Lord, don't let me draw another religious dry cell this afternoon. Must include the Swanns on my prayer list. They need help."

It happened the day after the Swanns arrived at the family camp. The morning schedule was about to begin. Young campers have a way of demonstrating that rising bells are unnecessary. Yesterday they had explored every building, run up and down every hill, broad jumped the creek, had their first swim. After a hearty dinner of stew and trimmings they were ready for games. Then, to bed, while the adults lingered at the campfire for songs and small talk. With the dawn, the children were at it again, but only briefly. Their shrill cries of alarm soon brought every adult into the open whether garbed for day or night, ready to meet the heralded emergency. Eyes followed wildly pointing fingers to the top of the hill. This was no "wolf-call." Clouds of smoke were beginning to rise ominously from the tall grass. Fanned by a strong south wind, the fire was reaching out in the direction of a grove of young pines, beyond which stood the cabins. It appeared as if the entire camp might be threatened. In a matter of seconds, David Thorpe had assumed the unforeseen role of fire marshal. Men were armed with axes and shovels. Women and older children formed a water brigade with every available pail and pan. The objective was to clear a corridor between the trees and the onrushing grassfire. Bill noted with what power and skill Thorpe applied his axe to bush and tree. Grass and earth were soaked with water some distance ahead of the approaching wall of flame. Soon, however, it became apparent to all that these well-meant efforts would be futile.

Then a strange thing happened. Suddenly, as if a great fan had been shut off, the wind ceased. The flames lost their fury. With renewed hope the laborers returned to their task. In a few moments, almost as suddenly as it had abated, the wind returned but from the opposite direction, carrying the diminishing flames back across the charred field. The grove was safe—and the camp. Weary and begrimed, but relieved, the camp sat down to breakfast. It was a different camp. Whatever of reserve and aloofness remained from the previous evening, was now gone. First names prevailed. All were as one family from that moment on. An emergency had accomplished in human relationships what five families and a priest had thus far been unable to achieve—unity.

Bill was to discover other things. Curt Norson and Jim Beck were fishermen like himself. Thorpe, a former college athlete, was good at any sport. Kramer and Staley liked photography, bridge, and golf. Several of them, including Bill and son, learned their first lessons in stone polishing. Strange but fortunate that these families should come to a church camp to discover how much they had in common.

Camp Carson narrows at its northern extremity to form a hilltop triangle. Here, on the ridge overlooking Trout Lake, campers gather for Vespers. The Rev. David Thorpe's brief talk focused on the events of the morning.

"All of us are thankful to God," he said, "that we have come to the end of this day without injury and without great loss. I wonder whether you thought, as I did, that the hand of God was in that situation this morning. Work as hard as we could, our efforts would have been meaningless except for one thing—the change of the wind. There is a lesson in that experience for all of us. How many times in life human efforts alone are inadequate. Then extra help comes from somewhere. There are those who refer to such incidents as "chance" or "luck." I don't. This morning God was in action in our behalf. He does not do our work for us; far from it. It is He who has given us both privilege and responsibility. He crowns our best efforts with His Grace. He created us to be dependent on Himself and upon one another." His eyes glanced down at the little faces at his feet, upturned to his own face. "These children are ours by His gift. Yet the gift carries with it a responsibility. Not only their physical lives, but their spiritual growth depend upon our care and nurture. We are stewards of a precious trust. We do not own them. So we must discover the design of the Giver for them and dedicate ourselves to its fulfillment. Yet without His help and guidance we are inadequate for such a task."

Thorpe's mind reached back to his daily ministry in the city—to the hospitals whose patients had been remembered by name but a few minutes ago. "Life is a gift of God," he continued. "When sickness comes, we entrust ourselves to those He has blessed with special skills, and whose dedication and development of those gifts makes them physicians. Yet, skilled as a surgeon may be, his efforts are futile except for God's additional gift of health to the patient." He went on, "We are stewards of our own lives. Some of us may feel that we do very well with them. According to the standards of our set and of our time, this may be true for a while. But the question is what is God's purpose for my life, or yours? For what were they designed? We cannot begin to make full use of them without His help, His Love, and His Grace . . ."

Bill Swann stared at the fieldstone altar, and beyond it, to the surface of the lake. Stewardship, Grace—these are unfamiliar terms to him. He thought of the northwind without which, a fire would have seared black this very spot. He thought of his own son, who in nine years of childhood had survived countless near-accidents, any one of which might have been fatal. It seemed to him in these moments, that Billie's life hung by a slender thread, given to him, the father, to hold. Just as this boy is completely dependent on him for physical life, so he must depend on his parents for values, ideals, character, and for purpose. What purpose—his or God's? Stewardship . . . Grace . . .

Coffeebreaks come often at family camp. The longest and best is the one before "taps." With the children safely in bed, conversation usually runs from the laughs of the day, to regrets or plans for the morrow. Tonight is an exception. Perhaps it was the morning's near tragedy—or the talk at Vespers—or the growing sense of fellowship that comes "where two or three are gathered together in His name." Curt Norson began, "Padre, I know what you were talking about tonight—this business of Grace or Help, or whatever you call it. Hope you don't mind my telling this, Dave." "Of course not, if you want to share it with us," was the reply. Curt continued, "Three years ago I was a wreck, physically, emotionally, every other way. I knew I had ulcers, began hitting the bottle, was behind in the payments on my house. Mae was ready to leave me; the kids were nervous and upset . . ." This was a successful junior executive speaking. Everyone listened in amazement, Bill Swann especially. He recognized a few of these symptoms in himself. Curt's story continues, "Then, to crown it all, I lost my job. When a man who always counted on his own ability, needs help, what does he do? I thought of several things, but I guess I made the right decision for once. I was going home; but I couldn't face Mae. Found myself in front of St. Paul's Church. That did it. I'd talk to Dave Thorpe. He takes care of my kids on Sunday. Used to know him in Korea. Told him the whole story. It was tough. What he made me do was harder still. Told me the best thing about me was the fact that I knew I needed help—and the next best thing was, that I wasn't blaming anyone but myself. First, we went into the church and asked for God's help. Then he went home with me to tell Mae. She was swell about it. By this time I began to feel as if a great weight had been lifted from my shoulders. Well, you probably can guess the rest—doctors, a psychiatrist, some long discussions with Dave—some 'will' power, some 'won't' power. Then Dave offered me a job—not for pay, mind you, but something to draw my attention away from Curt Norson. He put me to work counting Sunday offerings." Finally after considerable time I was ready to ask for my old job. Well, it took guts; and we lived on a shoestring for a while. . . . I hadn't intended to make a confession when I started. I just want to add this. When a guy discovers he can't do it alone, and that he has no right to live for himself alone, and when he offers what he is to God for His work, things begin to happen."

Jim Beck circled the table. He shook Curt's hand. "Guess we all needed this," he said. "We get caught in the web of the popular concerns—status, pride and pleasure, and we forget the real reasons for living."

"And the Help that's available," Mae added. Bill glanced at the mantle clock. Beneath it, carved in stone he read, "I'm Third."

Before the evening ended, the family campers discovered that family prayer after coffee is sometimes a good idea.

Bill Swann hurried home from work. Several things must be done before evening. Plans for the new classrooms at St. Paul's must be checked for cost before the meeting. But first, November's initial snowfall must be removed from sidewalk and driveway. The shovel in his hand reminded him of the last time he had used one. It was during the fire at the family camp. Never could he forget that week—and to think he almost missed it.

Bill and Dolores were frequent guests these days at the

Norsons. Together they had organized a parents discussion group. As Bill put it, "That camp put me straight on so many ideas I had all wrong that I'd like to see a lot more guys like me find some solid answers to the important questions. After all, how can we teach our youngsters to be Christians unless we have some grasp of the real meaning of it ourselves, and unless we start living like Christians?" He had pondered much over that slogan above the camp fireplace: "I'm Third." Gradually he was putting this simple arithmetic into his homelife: "God first, Dee and the children second, William Swann third." Once he might have asked, "What do I get out of it?" Three months of living by this rule made the answer unnecessary and the question irrelevant.

"Dinner!" That welcome call ended his meditation. Suddenly he was aware of his hunger. But in his heart he knew that a deeper "hunger" already was being satisfied. He was thinking of much more than food as the family gathered for the evening meal—blessings of home, the joy of children, companionship with Dolores such as he had never dreamed possible, new friends, life with meaning.

With bowed heads the Swanns said Grace together—a custom they unconsciously acquired at family camp:

For these and all His many blessings, God's Holy Name be praised, through Jesus Christ our Lord. *Amen.*

There is little doubt but that the unseen, yet welcome, Guest was listening.